ENGLISH IN TOURISM

May I Help You?

Christopher St J Yates

CASSELL

CASSELL PUBLISHERS LIMITED
Villiers House, 41/47 Strand
LONDON WC2N 5JE

First published 1991

British Library Cataloguing in Publication Data
Yates, C. St J. (Christopher St John)
   May I help you: a course for restaurant and bar staff.—
   (English in tourism).
   1. English language. Usage
   I. Title   II. Series
   428

   ISBN 0–304–33003–5

The Publishers gratefully acknowledge permission to use illustrative material from Holiday Inns International.

Illustrations by Peter Bull and Pan Tek Arts
Printed and bound in Great Britain
by Page Bros, Norwich.

CONTENTS

INTRODUCTION FOR STUDENTS

Read this before you begin the book!

I WHAT YOU NEED

May I Help You? gives you the English you need to do your job.

To use *May I Help You?* you need

- this book
- the cassettes
- a cassette recorder
- a dictionary

2 THE BOOK

In this book there is

- **The working material**
  This is what you learn from.

- **Keys and tapescripts**
  This is where you look for the right answers to the exercises. The tapescripts tell you what is on the cassettes.

- **A grammar**
  This explains what you are learning.

- **Notes for teachers**
  Do not use this.

3 HOW TO USE THE BOOK

There are two kinds of exercise. One with the cassettes and one without the cassettes. The exercises with the cassettes are marked:

- **Exercises without the cassettes**
  a Read the heading.
  b Read the instructions.
  c Look at the exercise.
  d If you understand, do the exercise.
  e If you do not understand, use your dictionary and the grammar. Ask a friend.
  f Look in the Key and check your answers.
  g Go on to the next exercise.

- **Exercises with the cassettes**
  a Read the heading.
  b Read the instructions.

c Look at the exercise.

d If you understand, turn on the cassette and do the exercise.

e If you do not understand, use a dictionary or ask a friend.

f If you do not understand the cassette look in the tapescript. Use your dictionary. Start the exercise again.

g Look in the Key and check your answers.

4 HOW TO WORK

Do not try to do too much at one time. Thirty minutes is a good time to spend each day.

If you do not understand an exercise, ask a friend to help you.

Learn the words you need.

Use what you learn in your work!

Enjoy the book!

INTRODUCTION FOR TEACHERS

I THE STUDENTS

May I Help You? teaches the basic language required by bar and restaurant staff within the hotel and catering industry. It is a companion course to *Check In*, which is for front office staff.

The materials are based on the relevant parts of the ICC* specifications for the hotel/catering industry.

May I Help You? and *Check In* are designed as self-access materials, as many, if not most, employees within the hotel/catering industry are not able to attend regular classes due to the hours they have to work.

2 THE MATERIALS

The materials consist of

- this book
- two cassettes

Students who may miss some lessons due to their working hours should also have a dictionary.

3 COURSE STRUCTURE

The course consists of ten Units. Each Unit normally consists of six pages, divided into two stages.

a Pen-to-paper
This stage introduces new language for the students to absorb and practise.
b Cassette work
This stage involves work with the cassettes and is where the new language is recycled, together with language from previous Units. The exercises consist of 'on-the-job' tasks, such as taking orders for meals and drinks.

For the benefit of self-access students, full keys to the exercises and tapescripts are provided after the working materials. There is also a simple grammar explaining the point of the various exercises.

4 ASSUMED KNOWLEDGE

The course assumes some previous contact with English, either at school or through the workplace. While minimal knowledge is assumed, this is not an absolute beginners' course.

5 LENGTH OF COURSE

This will depend substantially on the existing level of English of your class when starting the course. Depending on this, the course will provide a minimum of 30 lessons, rising to 60 for weaker classes.

* ICC—International Certificate Conference, a group of countries who have agreed common specifications and examinations for those working in the hotel/catering industry.

6 USE OF THE MATERIALS

While this book is designed mainly as a self-access course, it can also be used successfully in a teacher-directed class with teachers extending and personalising the course content. With a little imagination, other lively and enjoyable sessions can be developed where students are encouraged to build on their experiences. The following are a few suggestions for achieving this.

Personalise

Students can be encouraged to use knowledge of their own work situation in extensions of the coursebook exercises; for example, in Exercise 1 of Unit 1 students can describe their own jobs to the class. Students can bring realia, such as menus, bar tariffs and restaurant and hotel floor plans from their own work places and use these in group question and answer sessions. Students can recount situations where they have been required to give advice or to deal with complaints.

Where students are not yet working in the industry, teachers could ask students to prepare for individual lessons by finding out relevant information from a nearby hotel.

Increase oral content

Instead of writing responses to exercises in the book, students could answer orally or teachers could devise their own oral exercises, reserving those in the book for consolidation and homework. Oral responses could be made in a full class situation with the teacher playing the guest or, if students are confident, with students working in pairs.

Supplement

The book material can be supplemented with local material such as menus and maps collected by teacher and students. Why not even use real vegetables in Unit 5?

Exercises can also be supplemented by teacher-devised questions and situations similar to those in the book.

Extend

Teachers can develop exercises that challenge the students to go beyond the scope of this book. For example, situations can be extended through role play, initially with the teacher playing guest and the class responding. Later, as they gain confidence, students can work in groups with some acting parts and others observing and commenting. Finally, students can work in pairs or small groups with all students participating actively.

Depending on the ability of the students, situations can be made more difficult than those presented in the book, requiring the students to make more complex replies. They can also be asked to take down messages from the cassette tape without using the prompts in the book.

Practise pronunciation

Teachers can use the exercises in this book to provide formal pronunciation practice and can also use such things as menus and tariff cards for practice of individual words.

Provide pre-listening opportunities

Students can be prepared for the taped listening exercises by introducing them to any vocabulary which teachers have identified as likely to be unknown and by practising any difficult pronunciation. Teachers could also devise their own mini-situations, similar to the taped exercises, for acting out before the taped situation.

1 What do they do?

Look at the pictures below. They show people who work in the Holiday Inn hotel in Manchester, England.

1 Chef   2 Waitress   3 Receptionist   4 Porter

5 Cashier   6 Barman   7 Maid   8 Head waiter

Say what jobs these people do, like this:

1	*He's a chef.*
2	*She's*
3	
4	
5	
6	
7	
8	

Now say what these people do. Use the table below to help you.

The chef		all over the hotel.	He carries the luggage.
The waitress		in the bar.	She cleans them.
The receptionist		in the bedrooms.	He supervises the waiters.
The porter	*works*	at the front desk.	*He cooks the food.*
The cashier	works	in the restaurant.	She serves the meals.
The barman		*in the kitchen.*	She prepares the bills.
The maid		in the restaurant.	He serves the drinks.
The head waiter			She welcomes the guests.

9 *The chef works in the kitchen. He cooks the food.*

10	
11	
12	
13	
14	
15	
16	

2 In the restaurant

Look at this table in the restaurant in the Holiday Inn, Manchester.

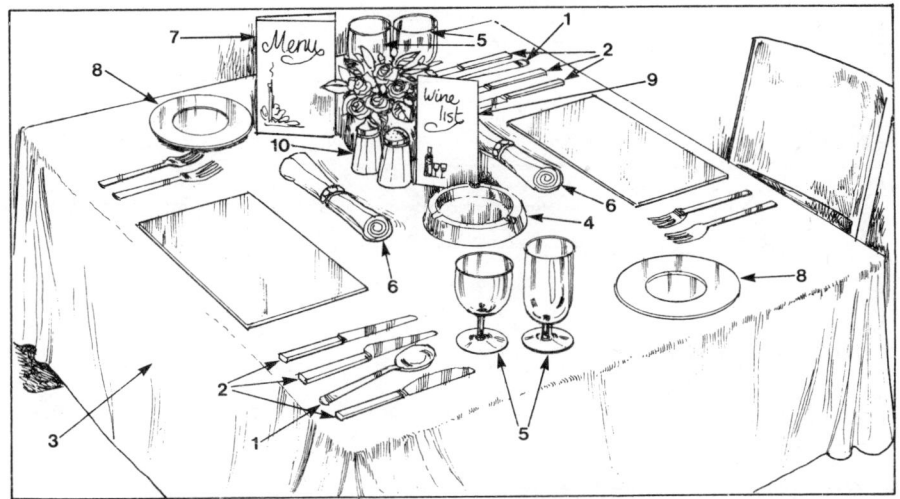

Now say what each place has got. Also say what there is on the table, like this:

Each place has got two forks. OR *There are two forks for each place.*

1	
2	
3	
4	
5	
6	
7	
8	
9	
10	

Now look at this table. Say what is wrong with it, like this:

The places haven't got any knives. OR *There aren't any knives.*
It hasn't got an ashtray. OR *There isn't an ashtray.*

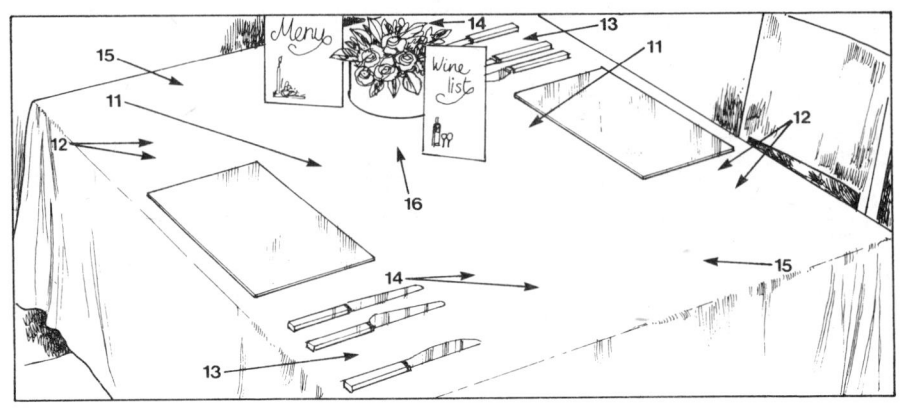

11 _____

12 _____

13 _____

14 _____

15 _____

16 _____

3 *What do you say?*

Look at these pictures and read the sentences. Then match the picture with the correct sentence, like this:

1 e _____

2 _____

3 _____

4 _____

5 _____

6 _____

a May (OR Can I) take your order, sir?
b May (OR Can I) give you the wine list, sir?
c May (OR Can I) get you a drink, sir?
d May (OR Can I) give you the menu, madam?
e May (OR Can I) get you a table, sir?
f May (OR Can I) take your coat, madam?

4 Tell the guest the way

Look at this plan of a hotel. You work in the restaurant in this hotel. Some guests want you to tell them where some of the hotel facilities are. Tell them the way, like this:

GUEST: Can you tell me where the cafeteria is, please?
YOU: *Certainly, sir. Turn left out of the restaurant and the cafeteria is on your left.*

Bank	Travel Agent		Disco	

Taxi rank

	Main entrance			
		Boutique		
Reception		Lifts	Bar	Lounge
	Foyer			

Cafeteria		Hairdresser	Night club

Restaurant

Now complete these sentences.

1 GUEST: Can you tell me the way to the lounge, please?

YOU: Certainly, madam. Turn _____ out of the res-taurant. Go past the bar and the lounge is on your _____.

2 GUEST: Can you tell me if there's a bank near here?

YOU: _____, madam. Go across the foyer and _____ the main entrance. Cross the street, go _____ the travel agent and the bank is _____ _____.

3 GUEST: Can you tell me where the night club is, please?

YOU: Certainly, sir. _____ the restaurant. Go _____ the hairdresser and the night club is _____.

4 GUEST: Do you know if there's a disco near here?

YOU: _____, sir. Go _____ the foyer and out of the _____. _____ the street and the disco is _____.

5 GUEST: Do you know where the boutique is?

YOU: Certainly, madam. _____ the restaurant. _____ the foyer and the _____ is on your right.

5 What does the guest want?

Peter works in the Holiday Inn, Manchester. Guests order food and drinks from him. Listen to the guests' orders. Then read the answers below. Listen to the question again, and put a tick ☑ against the right answer.

1 The guest wants
  a to know the way to room 21. ☐
  b a bottle of white wine in the restaurant. ☐
  c a bottle of white wine in his room. ☐

2 The guest wants
  a a glass of iced water. ☐
  b a whisky without ice. ☐
  c a whisky with ice. ☐

3 The guest wants
  a melon. ☐
  b soup. ☐
  c salad. ☐

4 The guest wants
  a an omelette. ☐
  b fish. ☐
  c a steak. ☐

5 The guest wants
  a a gin and tonic and then rosé wine. ☐
  b just an aperitif. ☐
  c a gin and tonic and then red wine. ☐

6 Conversations

Here are some conversations. Listen to the conversations and follow them in your book. Then rewind your cassette. Start the conversation again. This time, speak to the guest at the same time as the voice on the cassette.

WAITER: Good evening, madam. Good evening, sir.
GUEST: Good evening. A table for two, please.
WAITER: Certainly, sir. This way, please.
GUEST: Thank you.

WAITER:	Is this all right for you, sir?
GUEST:	Fine, thanks.
WAITER:	Can I get you an aperitif, sir?
GUEST:	Yes, my wife will have a tomato juice and I'll have a gin and tonic.
WAITER:	Thank you, sir.
GUEST 1:	Ah, good.
WAITRESS:	Good evening, gentlemen. May I give you the menu?
GUEST 1:	Thank you. Are you going to have something first, George?
GUEST 2:	A whisky with ice. On the rocks, that is.
GUEST 3:	I'll have the same.
WAITRESS:	That's two whiskies on the rocks. Thank you.
GUEST 1:	Right, now let's have a look at what . . .

7 *Offering food and drink*

 Look at the menu below.

STARTERS

Prawn cocktail
Pâté de maison
Soup of the day
Fresh melon
Smoked salmon
Salade Niçoise

****

MAIN COURSE

Lamb cutlets
Fillet steak
Sole
Omlette (ham,
tomato, mushroom)
Chicken Kiev
Salad (ham,
beef, chicken)

WINE LIST

GERMANY

Baden Dry
Piesporter Michelsberg
Geisenheimer Schlossgarten
Franken Sylvaner
Niersteiner Domtal
Goldener Oktober Riesling

FRANCE

WHITE

Bordeaux Blanc de Blancs
Chablis, 1983

ROSE

Anjou Rosé

RED

Le Piat de Beaujolais
Côtes du Rhone
Mouton Cadet

Now look at these sentences. When you have done that, turn on your cassette recorder. You will hear some guests. Choose the sentence which answers the guest. Say the sentence onto the cassette. You will then hear the right answer.

Would you like the Baden dry, sir, or perhaps the Piesporter?
Would you like the Anjou Rosé, madam?
Would you like the smoked salmon, madam?
Would you like the soup, madam?
Would you like the fillet steak, sir?
Would you like the omelette, madam?
Would you like a salad, sir?
Would you like the Bordeaux Blanc de Blancs, madam, or perhaps the Chablis?

8 *Take the order*

Now listen to these guests. They are ordering their meals. Look at the menu on page 6 and write down the orders.

Holiday Inn

1 _____

_____

_____

2 _____

3 _____

_____

_____

4 _____

_____

_____

5 _____

_____

_____

6 _____

_____

_____

UNIT 2

1 *What do you say?*

Look at these pictures and read the sentences. Then match the pictures with the correct sentence.

1 _____ 2 _____ 3 _____

4 _____ 5 _____ 6 _____

a Would you like me to fill your glass, sir?
b Would you like to see the wine list, sir?
c Would you like to sit outside, madam?
d Would you like to help yourself, madam?
e Would you like me to take your coat, madam?
f Would you like to follow me, madam?

2 *Asking questions*

Anna works in the restaurant in the Holiday Inn, Frankfurt. She must often ask the guests questions. Complete her sentences below. Use these words:

What	When	Where	How	Who

1 _____ would you like to sit, sir?
2 _____ would you like your steak done, madam?
3 _____ did you make your reservation, sir? Last night?
4 _____ time do you want your table for, madam?
5 _____ is your room number, sir?

8

6 _____ did you speak to about this, madam?

7 _____ many guests are you expecting, sir?

8 _____ would you like to pay, madam?

9 _____ would you like to drink, sir?

10 _____ did you leave your coat, madam? In the cloakroom?

3 Answering questions

Anna must also answer the guests' questions. Use the table below and answer the guests' questions.

It We They	close(s) open(s) don't charge cost(s) sell offer buy don't allow accept serve	cigarettes in the foyer. most credit cards. light meals in the cafeteria. eighteen marks. all our vegetables fresh. at 9.30. at two in the morning. for service. set menus as well. pets in the restaurant.

1 How much is breakfast?

_____

2 What time does the bar close?

_____

3 How much do you add for service?

_____

4 What time do the banks open round here?

_____

5 Can I get some cigarettes here?

_____

6 Can I bring my dog into the restaurant?

_____

7 Do you take credit cards?

_____

8 I don't want a full meal. Just an omelette or something. Can I get that here?

_____

9 Is your restaurant all à la carte?

_____

10 Are these peas out of a can?

_____

4 Answer the guests' questions

Read the guests' questions below. Then answer their questions. Use the words from the list below. Notice that the **answers** are in the **past**.

take	reserve	think	*arrive*	close	order	ask	wait
		put	leave				

1 Is Mr Loewenthal here yet, do you know?
He _arrived_ ten minutes ago, sir.

2 Is the cafeteria still open by any chance?
It _____ half an hour ago, I'm afraid, madam.

3 Where can I find Mr Gonzalez?
He _____ you to meet him in the bar, sir.

4 I think I left my briefcase here. Have you got it?
I _____ it in the cloakroom for you, sir.

5 Is a Miss Larsson still here? I'm very late, I know.
Miss Larsson _____ for half an hour, sir, and then _____.

6 My name's Jones. I booked a table for two.
I _____ a table for you by the window, madam.

7 And about time too. What happened?
I'm sorry about the delay, sir. It _____ longer than I _____
to change your order.

8 I don't think that fish is mine, you know.
I'm sorry, madam. I thought you _____ fish.

5 Asking the guest questions

Read what these guests say. Then ask them a question, like this:

1 But I'm sure I _made_ a reservation.
When _did you make_ it, sir?

2 This isn't what I ordered, you know.
I'm sorry, madam. What _____?

3 I'm sure I left it on the table.
What _____ on the table, sir?

4 I've already paid my bill.
I see, sir. How _____ it?

5 I spoke to someone about having a table by the window.
Who _____ to, madam?

6 Saying no politely

Sometimes you must say *no* to a guest. Read what these guests say, and then answer, like this:

1 But I phoned you and changed the time. Didn't you get the message?
No, sir/madam, I'm sorry. I'm afraid we didn't get it.

2 Did you find my handbag last night?

3 But didn't you know we would be six for dinner?

4 But my friend gave you the message, I'm sure.

5 My colleague rang you last night about our reservation.

7 In the bar

Read through the bar list on the next page. Then turn on your cassette. Some guests are ordering drinks. Listen to their orders. Then read the answers in your book. Listen to the order again, and put a tick ☑ against the right order.

1 The guest wants
  a a Dubonnet. ☐
  b a Martini. ☐
  c a Cinzano. ☐

2 The guest wants
  a a proprietary gin. ☐
  b a regular gin and tonic. ☐
  c a regular gin and orange. ☐

3 The guest wants
  a a proprietary vodka. ☐
  b a regular vodka. ☐
  c a Stolichnaya. ☐

4 The guest wants
  a a rye whisky. ☐
  b a regular scotch. ☐
  c a bourbon. ☐

5 The guest wants
  a an ice cream. ☐
  b a lemonade. ☐
  c a Perrier with ice and lemon. ☐

6 The guest wants
  a a Martell 3 Star. ☐
  b a Remy Martin 3 Star. ☐
  c a Remy Martin VSOP. ☐

7 The guest wants
  a a Croft Original. ☐
  b a Tio Pepe. ☐
  c a Bristol Cream. ☐

8 The guest wants a glass of
  a rosé wine. ☐
  b red wine. ☐
  c white wine. ☐

BAR LIST

WHISKY	MIXERS & MINERALS
Scotch Proprietary	Baby Mixers
Scotch Regular	Baby Juices
Irish	Coke
Rye	Perrier 220 ml
Bourbon	Splits
Malt & Deluxe	

GIN — **APERITIFS**

WHISKY

Scotch Proprietary
Scotch Regular
Irish
Rye
Bourbon
Malt & Deluxe

GIN
Proprietary
Regular

VODKA
Proprietary
Regular
Stolichnaya

RUM
Commodore
Bacardi

COGNAC (1/6 Gill)
Louis Bernard
Martell 3 Star
Remy Martin 3 Star
Remy Martin VSOP

ARMAGNAC (1/6 Gill)
Janneau 1961

LIQUEURS

MIXERS & MINERALS
Baby Mixers
Baby Juices
Coke
Perrier 220 ml
Splits

APERITIFS
Willoughbys Special No. 20 Port
Grahams White Port
Warres 1975 Vintage Port
Willoughbys Sherries
Tio Pepe
Croft Original
Bristol Cream
Campari
Pernod/Ricard

VERMOUTHS
Dubonnet
Martini/Cinzano

WINE
House per Glass

CHAMPAGNE
House per Glass

GIN, WHISKY, VODKA, RUM ARE SERVED IN MEASURES OF 1/3 GILL OR MULTIPLES THEREOF

NOTES: 'Proprietary' here means 'of the hotel'; the hotel's own brand. Tio Pepe, Croft Original and Bristol Cream are kinds of sherry. 'Regular' means a named brand, like Gordon's (gin), The Famous Grouse (whisky).

8 *Conversations*

Here are some conversations. Listen to the conversations and follow them in your book. Then rewind your cassette. Start the conversation again. This time, speak to the guest at the same time as the voice on the cassette.

BARMAN: Good evening, sir. What would you like?

GUEST: What kinds of whisky have you got?

BARMAN: We've got our own brand, sir. Or I can give you an Irish whisky, a rye, a bourbon or a malt.

GUEST: I'll have a malt. A double, please.

BARMAN: Certainly, sir. Would you like any water or ice with it?

GUEST: No water, thank you. That spoils it. I'll have just one lump of ice.

BARMAN: One lump, sir. Certainly.

BARMAN: Good evening, madam. Can I get you something to drink?

GUEST: Yes, you certainly can. I'd like a gin, please.

BARMAN: What would you like with it, madam?

GUEST:	Oh, let me see. Tonic, please.
BARMAN:	A gin and tonic. Would you like ice and lemon with it?
GUEST:	Yes, please.

BARMAN:	Good evening, gentlemen. What can I get for you?
GUEST 1:	What about you, Henry?
GUEST 2:	Cognac for me. Let's look at the tariff here. Ah, not a cognac. I'll have the armagnac.
GUEST 1:	And you, Peter?
GUEST 3:	Vodka. A Stolichnaya.
GUEST 1:	And I'll have a large bourbon. Just as it comes, no ice or anything.
BARMAN:	Certainly, sir. That's an armagnac, a Stolichnaya and a large bourbon. There's ice on the bar there, if you want any.
GUEST 1:	OK.

9 *Offering drinks*

 Now look at these sentences. When you have done that, turn on your cassette recorder. You will hear some guests. Choose the sentence which answers the guest. Say the sentence onto the cassette. You will then hear the right answer.

> Would you like a Pernod or a sherry, sir?
> Would you like a Tio Pepe, a Croft Original or a Bristol Cream, sir?
> Would you like a Cinzano or a Martini, madam?
> Would you like a juice or a mineral water, madam?
> Would you like bourbon, rye or malt, sir?
> Would you like a Louis Bernard, a Martell or a Remy Martin, madam?

10 *Take the order*

 Now listen to these guests. They are ordering drinks. Look again at the bar list on page 12 and use the page opposite to write down the guests' orders.

1

2

3

4

5

6

UNIT 3

1 Asking questions

Look at these pictures and read the sentences. Then match the pictures with the correct sentence.

1 _____   2 _____   3 _____

4 _____   5 _____   6 _____

a Have you seen the menu, sir?
b Have you lost a handbag, madam?
c Have you reserved a table, madam?

d Have you finished, sir?
e Have you tasted the wine, sir?
f Have you chosen the wine, madam?

2 Some more questions

Sometimes you want to ask your guest a question. Write questions using *Have* or *Has*, like this:

Order a sweet?
Have you ordered a sweet, sir/madam?

1 Lose your wallet?

_____

2 Book a table?

_____

3 Choose the wine?

_____

4 Your guest come?

_____

5 Your son finish?

_____

6 Your daughter have enough?

_____

What's the best answer?

Look at what these guests say to you. Then choose the best answer from the table below, like this:

I don't smoke.
I've reserved a table in the no smoking area, sir/madam.

I've	ordered arranged reserved put left told	a message in reception, madam. the barman to charge everything to you, sir. a table by the window, madam. for them to play it at 9, sir. you in the corner, sir. a special meal for him, madam.

1 I wanted a table with a view.

_____

2 I asked for a nice, quiet table.

_____

3 Do my guests know that they should meet me here?

_____

4 This is our anniversary. Do the band know about our tune?

_____

5 You do know my husband needs special food?

_____

6 I don't want my guests to pay for their drinks.

_____

Some short answers

Sometimes you don't need to answer your guest with a full sentence. Use short answers with these guests, like this:

Has my guest arrived?
No, sir/madam, I'm afraid he/she hasn't.

1 Have you seen a small girl in a red dress?

_____

2 Have my friends come?

_____

3 Has my wife arrived yet?

_____

4 Has the bar opened yet?

_____

5 Have you found my coat yet?

_____

5 He may have gone to reception

Jean works in the restaurant of the Holiday Inn in Paris. Sometimes people ask him questions which he cannot answer. But he tries to be helpful, like this:

Where can I find Mr Reynolds?
go/reception
I don't know, sir/madam. He may/could have gone to reception.

1 Do you know where my husband is?
go/bar

_____

2 Why isn't Mr Georgiou here?
cancel/reservation

_____

3 I was expecting Mrs Hussein here this evening. Has she been in?
eat/room

_____

4 I can't see Mr Gabbiadini. Is he here?
decide/go outside

_____

5 I left my umbrella here. Do you know where it's gone?
my colleague/take/cloakroom

_____

6 Where's Mr Le Tissier this evening?
leave/early

_____

6 Talking to guests

Complete the following sentences. Use these words:

somewhere	something	someone/somebody	nothing	no one/nobody
	nowhere	anywhere	anyone	anything

1 Your briefcase, sir? I'm afraid it isn't _____ in the bar.

2 The restaurant's full, sir. I'm afraid there's _____ we can do.

3 _____ left a message for you, madam. At reception.

4 Your guest, madam? I'm afraid _____ has seen him.

5 We'll page him, sir. I'm sure he's _____ in the hotel.

6 A table for 10, madam? I'm sure there's _____ we can arrange.

7 The other tables are reserved, madam. There's _____ else to sit.

8 I'm afraid we haven't got _____ else, sir. It's all on the menu.

9 There isn't _____ sitting here, madam. Would you like this table?

7 Room service

Read through the room service menu below. Then turn on your cassette. Some guests are ordering food. Listen to their orders. Then read the answers in your book. Listen to the order again and put a tick ☑ against the right order.

═══ROOM SERVICE═══

Soups

FRENCH ONION

•

CONSOMMÉ WITH MUSHROOMS, RAVIOLI AND HERBS

•

TOMATO

Snacks

HAMBURGER 'HOLIDAY INN' BACON, ONIONS, FRIED EGG FRENCH FRIES

•

RAGOUT OF CHICKEN AND FRESH MUSHROOMS SERVED IN A PASTRY CASE

•

CHEF'S SALAD, WITH CHEESE, HAM, EGG AND SHRIMPS

•

COLD ROAST BEEF WITH MIXED PICKLES, SAUCE REMOULADE AND ROAST POTATOES

Main dishes

ESCALOPE 'CORDON BLEU' WITH PEAS, CARROTS AND FRENCH FRIES

•

GRILLED MINUTE STEAK, SAUSAGE, BACON, BAKED POTATO, HERB BUTTER AND A MIXED SALAD

For children

FRIED FISH, WITH FRENCH FRIES AND A SMALL MIXED SALAD

•

GRILLED SAUSAGES WITH FRENCH FRIES

•

ESCALOPE OF PORK WITH FRENCH FRIES AND A SMALL MIXED SALAD

•

VEAL STEAK IN A CREAMED MUSHROOM SAUCE WITH RICE THREE FLAVOUR ICE-CREAM ON FRUIT COCKTAIL TOPPED WITH WHIPPED CREAM

1 The guest wants
  a French onion soup. ☐
  b consommé. ☐
  c tomato soup. ☐

2 The guest wants
  a one French onion soup. ☐
  b two consommés. ☐
  c two French onion soups. ☐

3 The guest wants
  a the Chef's salad. ☐
  b cold roast beef. ☐
  c a hamburger. ☐

4 The guest wants
  a ragoût and a Chef's salad. ☐
  b cold roast beef and a
    hamburger. ☐
  c cold roast beef and ragoût. ☐

5 The guest wants
  a escalope 'Cordon Bleu' and a
    steak. ☐
  b a steak and an escalope of
    pork. ☐
  c a minute steak and a ragoût. ☐

6 The guest wants
  a a veal steak and fried fish. ☐
  b sausages and an escalope of
    pork. ☐
  c a veal steak and grilled
    sausages. ☐

7 The guest wants
  a fried fish and a ragoût. ☐
  b a steak and fried fish. ☐
  c an ice cream and fried fish. ☐

8 The guest wants
  a French onion soup and a
    hamburger. ☐
  b a hamburger. ☐
  c tomato soup and a hamburger. ☐

8 Some conversations

Here are some conversations. Listen to the conversations and follow them in your book. Then rewind your cassette. Start the conversation again. This time, speak to the guest at the same time as the voice on the cassette. Here's the first conversation.

GUEST: Is that room service?
WAITER: Yes, sir, it is.
GUEST: I haven't got a room service menu here in my room, but can you do me something cold?
WAITER: Certainly, sir. Why don't you try the Chef's salad? It's really very good.
GUEST: What's in it?
WAITER: It comes with cheese, ham, eggs and shrimps, sir.
GUEST: That sounds fine. I'll have that. Oh, and half a bottle of a dry white wine.
WAITER: And half a bottle of dry white wine. What is your room number, sir?
GUEST: 20.
WAITER: Thank you, sir.

WAITER: Room service, can I help you?
GUEST: Yes, I and my family would like to have supper in our rooms. We'd like, let's see, two tomato soups . . .
WAITER: Two tomato soups, madam.
GUEST: And two consommés.
WAITER: Two consommés.
GUEST: Then, for the children, the grilled sausages and a veal steak.
WAITER: One grilled sausages, one veal steak.
GUEST: And for us, the chicken and an escalope 'Cordon Bleu'.
WAITER: One ragoût of chicken and a 'Cordon Bleu'. Anything to drink, madam?
GUEST: No, thank you. That's all.
WAITER: Thank you, madam. What room number is it?
GUEST: 489.
WAITER: 489. It'll be about ten minutes.
GUEST: That's fine.

9 Making suggestions

 Now look at these sentences. When you have done that, turn on your cassette recorder. You will hear some guests. Choose the sentence that answers the guest. Say the sentence onto the cassette. You will then hear the right answer.

> Why don't you try the consommé, madam? It's really very good.
> Why don't you try the Chef's salad, sir? It's excellent.
> Why don't they try the sausages, madam? They're very good.
> Why don't you try the escalope 'Cordon Bleu', sir? It's excellent.
> Why don't they try the fried fish, sir? It comes with French fries and a small
>   mixed salad.
> Why don't you try the ice cream, madam? It's on a fruit cocktail topped with
>   whipped cream.

10 Take the order

 Now listen to these guests. They are ordering meals. Look at the menu and write down the orders and the room numbers.

Holiday Inn

1 _____

2 _____

3 _____

4 _____

5 _____

6 _____

UNIT 4

1 What do you say?

Look at these pictures and read the sentences. Then match the pictures with the correct sentences.

a I'll take it, madam.
b I'll get you the bill, sir.
c I'll fetch a cloth, sir.

d I'll bring it up immediately, madam.
e I'll get you the menu, sir.
f I'll take it away, madam.

2 Saying what you will do

Look at what these guests say. Use the table below, and say what you will do to help them.

I'll	get ask bring leave	another tablecloth, madam. the chef about it, sir. at reception for you, madam. you a clean one, sir. the wine waiter, madam. them to your table, sir. the trolley, madam. it in the cloakroom, sir.

1 This wine's off.

_____

2 This fish doesn't taste right to me, you know.

_____

3 I've dropped my knife on the floor.

_____

4 Can you put my briefcase somewhere?

_____

5 Would you help me carry these drinks?

_____

6 Are there any messages for me?

_____

7 I'd like a sweet, please.

_____

8 I'm sorry, my son's spilled his orange juice all over the table.

_____

3 Giving advice

Sometimes guests ask for advice. Look at what these guests say. Then give them advice, using the notes and one of the sentences, like this:

1 Is there anything to see in this city?
visit/old city
It's worth visiting the old city, sir/madam. It's very lively.

These are the sentences to use:

I'm sure they can help.	There are some lovely views.
It's really excellent.	It runs every half hour.
We get fairly full after 8 o'clock.	There's a very good cabaret.
It's very lively.	

2 Do I need to book?
reserve/table

_____

_____

3 Is there anything to do in the hotel after dinner?
visit/night club

_____

_____

4 Are there any sights near here?
see/castle

_____

_____

5 Is there a travel agent near here? I want to change my tickets.
ask/reception

_____

_____

6 What's the best way to the airport from here?
take/courtesy bus

_____

_____

7 What do you suggest as a main course?
try/chef's speciality

_____

_____

4 Asking what the guest prefers

Sometimes you need to ask guests what they prefer. You can do that like this:

I'd like some pâté, please.
Would you rather/prefer the pâté de campagne or the pâté maison, sir?

Now ask what these guests would prefer. Use the table below.

Would you	prefer rather	red or white, madam? draught or bottled, sir? the entrecôte or the tournedos, madam? cognac or armagnac, sir? mixed vegetable or tomato, madam?

1 I'll have a brandy, please.

_____

2 Some soup to start with, please.

_____

3 Could I have a glass of wine?

_____

4 I'd like a steak as the main course, I think.

_____

5 A beer, please.

_____

5 Offering to help

Look at these pictures and read the sentences. Then match the pictures with the correct sentence.

1 _____   2 _____   3 _____

4 _____   5 _____   6 _____

a Shall I get you an ashtray, madam?
b Shall I pour the wine now, sir?
c Shall I get the children's menu, madam?
d Shall I show you the way?
e Shall I get a more suitable chair, sir?
f Shall I open the wine now, sir?

6 The breakfast menu

Read through the breakfast menu on page 25. Then turn on your cassette. Some guests are ordering breakfast. Listen to their orders. Then read the answers in your book. Listen to the order again and put a tick ☑ against the right order.

1 The guest wants
  a the American breakfast. ☐
  b the Continental breakfast. ☐
  c the Healthy breakfast. ☐

2 The guest wants
  a scrambled eggs with ham. ☐
  b poached eggs with ham. ☐
  c scrambled eggs with bacon. ☐

3 The guest wants
  a orange juice, oatmeal and tea. ☐
  b tomato juice, yoghurt and tea. ☐
  c orange juice, yoghurt and tea. ☐

4 The guest wants
  a a mushroom omelette. ☐
  b a ham omelette. ☐
  c a cheese omelette. ☐

5 The guest wants
  a fried eggs. ☐
  b scrambled eggs. ☐
  c poached eggs. ☐

6 The guest wants
  a fried eggs and ham. ☐
  b poached eggs and bacon. ☐
  c fried eggs and bacon. ☐

7 The guest wants
  a toast. ☐
  b a Danish pastry. ☐
  c a croissant. ☐

8 The guest wants
  a tomato juice, oatmeal and tea. ☐
  b tomato juice, oatmeal and coffee. ☐
  c tomato juice, oatmeal and
    caffeine free coffee. ☐

AMERICAN BREAKFAST

Fruit juice...*Tomato, orange or grapefruit*

Two fresh eggs, any style ....*Fried, poached, boiled or scrambled*
...............................*with bacon, ham or sausage*

Croissant, toast or Danish pastry

Coffee or tea

CONTINENTAL BREAKFAST

Fruit juice...*Tomato, orange or grapefruit*

Croissant, toast or Danish pastry

Coffee or tea

HEALTHY BREAKFAST

Fruit juice...*Tomato, orange or grapefruit*

Oatmeal or Yoghurt

Vegetable salad

Toasted wheatgerm bread

Coffee, caffeine free coffee or tea

BEVERAGES

Fresh juice...*Orange or grapefruit*

Fruit juice...*Tomato, orange or grapefruit*

Coffee, tea

Milk, yoghurt

Hot chocolate

EGGS AND OMELETTES

Two fresh eggs, any style ....*Fried, boiled, scrambled or poached*

Omelettes.........................*Bacon, tomato, plain, cheese, mushroom or ham*

7 Some conversations

Here are some conversations. Listen to the conversations and follow them in your book. Then rewind your cassette. Start the conversation again. This time, speak to the guest at the same time as the voice on the cassette.

GUEST: Good morning. The American breakfast, please.
WAITRESS: Certainly, madam. Would you prefer tomato, orange or grapefruit juice?
GUEST: Oh, I think the grapefruit, please.
WAITRESS: How would you like your eggs?
GUEST: Fried, I think.
WAITRESS: And would you rather have bacon, ham or sausage, madam?
GUEST: Sausage, please. Oh, and tea.
WAITRESS: Would you like a croissant?
GUEST: No, I think the Danish pastry.
WAITRESS: Thank you, madam.

GUEST: Ah, good.
WAITRESS: What can I get you, sir?
GUEST: I'll have a fresh grapefruit juice.
WAITRESS: A fresh grapefruit juice, sir, yes.
GUEST: Coffee, and a cheese omelette.
WAITRESS: A cheese omelette. Anything else, sir?
GUEST: Er, yes, I'll have a yoghurt too.
WAITRESS: And a yoghurt. Thank you, sir.

GUEST: Morning.
WAITER: Good morning, sir.
GUEST: The Healthy breakfast, I think.
WAITER: Certainly, sir. And would you rather have tomato, orange or grapefruit juice?
GUEST: Orange, I think.
WAITER: Oatmeal or yoghurt, sir?
GUEST: Oatmeal, please. And coffee.
WAITER: With or without caffeine, sir?
GUEST: Without.
WAITER: Thank you, sir.

8 Wrong orders

Now look at these sentences. When you have done that, turn on your cassette recorder. You will now hear some guests. Choose the sentence that answers the guest. Say the sentence onto the cassette. You will then hear the right answer.

> I'll get you some coffee straightaway, sir.
> I'll get some boiled eggs immediately, sir.
> I'll get you an orange juice immediately, sir.
> I'll fetch you some fried eggs at once, madam.
> I'll fetch you a yoghurt straightaway, madam.
> I'll ask chef for a ham omelette at once, madam.

9 *Take the order*

Now listen to these guests. They are ordering meals. Look at the menu and write down the orders.

Holiday Inn

1 _____

2 _____

3 _____

4 _____

5 _____

6 _____

UNIT 5

1 How are they served?

Look at these pictures and read the sentences. The sentences tell you how the dishes are served. Match the pictures with the sentences.

1 _____ 2 _____ 3 _____

4 _____ 5 _____ 6 _____

a The shrimp cocktail is served with Aurora sauce.
b The scallops are sautéed in butter and served with bacon and mushrooms.
c The chicken is fried and served with chips and peas.
d The mussels are cooked in a white wine sauce.
e The steak is grilled and served with carrots and French fried potatoes.
f The roast beef is served with beans, roast potatoes and carrots.

2 How is it cooked?

These guests want to know how their meals are cooked. Answer their questions, using the notes, like this:

Is the chicken boiled? (fry)
No, sir/madam, it's fried. _____

1 Are the potatoes roasted? (boil)

_____

2 Is the steak fried? (grill)

_____

3 Are the eggs boiled? (poach)

_____

4 Is the trout fried? (bake)

_____

5 Does the fruit salad come with ordinary cream? (whip)

_____

3 Which vegetables?

Look at these vegetables and learn the English words.

peas

beans

spinach

cucumber

onions

brussels sprouts

broccoli

lettuce

beetroot

celery

cauliflower

leek

mushrooms

tomatoes

chips and roast potatoes

carrots

Now answer these guests' questions, like this:

What vegetables come with the steak?

It's served with peas, mushrooms, chips and tomatoes, sir/madam.

1 What do I get in the cold chicken salad?

_____

_____

_____

2 What vegetables come with the kidneys?

_____

_____

_____

3 What comes with the gammon steak?

_____

_____

_____

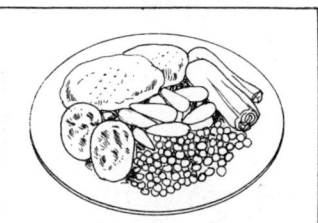

4 What do I get with the roast duck?

_____

_____

_____

5 What comes with the roast lamb?

_____

_____

_____

4 Where was it found?

Sometimes guests lose things or leave them in the restaurant. Ask these guests whether what you have found belongs to them, like this:

briefcase; find/under the table
Is this your briefcase, sir/madam? It was found under the table.

1 purse; find/on the table

_____

2 coats; leave/in the cloakroom

_____

3 wallet; deposit/at reception

_____

4 briefcase; discover/in the bar

_____

5 umbrella; hand in/to the lost property office

_____

6 mackintosh; put/over your chair

_____

5 A choice of vegetables

  Look at this list of vegetables. Guests can choose which vegetables they want. Listen to the guests ordering their vegetables, and put a tick ☑ against the ones they want.

SALAD VEGETABLES

Lettuce, cucumber, tomatoes, broad beans, runner beans, celery, beetroot, carrots.

VEGETABLES

Cabbage, peas, broad beans, runner beans, spinach, brussels sprouts, onions, broccoli, cauliflower, leeks, mushrooms, tomatoes, chips, roast potatoes, boiled potatoes

1 lettuce ☐ cucumber ☐ tomatoes ☐ broad beans ☐ runner beans ☐ celery ☐ beetroot ☐ carrots ☐

2 cabbage ☐ peas ☐ broad beans ☐ runner beans ☐ spinach ☐ brussels sprouts ☐ onions ☐ broccoli ☐ cauliflower ☐ leeks ☐ mushrooms ☐ tomatoes ☐ chips ☐ roast potatoes ☐ boiled potatoes ☐

3 lettuce ☐ cucumber ☐ tomatoes ☐ broad beans ☐ runner beans ☐ celery ☐ beetroot ☐ carrots ☐

4 cabbage ☐ peas ☐ broad beans ☐ runner beans ☐ spinach ☐ brussels sprouts ☐ onions ☐ broccoli ☐ cauliflower ☐ leeks ☐ mushrooms ☐ tomatoes ☐ chips ☐ roast potatoes ☐ boiled potatoes ☐

5 lettuce ☐ cucumber ☐ tomatoes ☐ broad beans ☐ runner beans ☐ celery ☐ beetroot ☐ carrots ☐ cabbage ☐ peas ☐ spinach ☐

6 brussels sprouts ☐ onions ☐ broccoli ☐ cauliflower ☐ leeks ☐ mushrooms ☐ tomatoes ☐ chips ☐ roast potatoes ☐ boiled potatoes ☐

7 lettuce ☐ cucumber ☐ tomatoes ☐ broad beans ☐ runner beans ☐ celery ☐ beetroot ☐ carrots ☐

8 cabbage ☐ peas ☐ broad beans ☐ runner beans ☐ spinach ☐ brussels sprouts ☐ onions ☐ broccoli ☐ cauliflower ☐ leeks ☐ mushrooms ☐ tomatoes ☐ chips ☐ roast potatoes ☐ boiled potatoes ☐

6 *Some conversations*

 Here are some conversations. Listen to the conversations and follow them in your book. Then rewind your cassette. Start the conversation again. This time, speak to the guest at the same time as the voice on the cassette.

WAITRESS: What would you like to go with that, sir? As vegetables.

GUEST: I'd like some boiled potatoes. And then, well, what would you recommend?

WAITRESS: I suggest the broccoli, sir. It's in season at the moment, and is very good.

GUEST: Right, broccoli, and one more. I know, I'll have peas.

WAITRESS: And some peas. Anything else, sir?

GUEST: No, that'll do fine, thanks.

WAITRESS: Thank you, sir.

GUEST: Now, vegetables to go with my steak. Are the tomatoes grilled, by the way?

WAITER: Yes, madam, they're grilled.

GUEST: Tomatoes, then, and onions, if they're fried.

WAITER: Fried onions.

GUEST: With some chips and runner beans, I think.

WAITER: Chips and runner beans. Thank you, madam.

GUEST: Have I understood this right? I choose what I want to go with a ham salad, and then the chef makes it up?

WAITRESS: That's quite right, madam.

GUEST: Then I'll have beetroot and . . .

WAITRESS: Beetroot, madam. And what else would you like?

GUEST: Carrots.

WAITRESS: Carrots.

GUEST: Lettuce and tomato, I think.

WAITRESS: Lettuce and tomato. Thank you, madam.

7 Making suggestions

 These guests cannot decide what vegetables to have. Suggest what they should have, using the pictures below. First listen to this example:

GUEST: What's good at the moment in the way of vegetables?

YOU: *I should have the broad beans and the spinach, sir. They're both in season at the moment.*

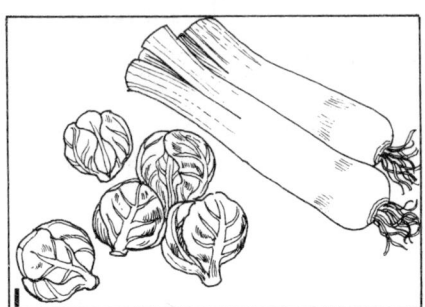

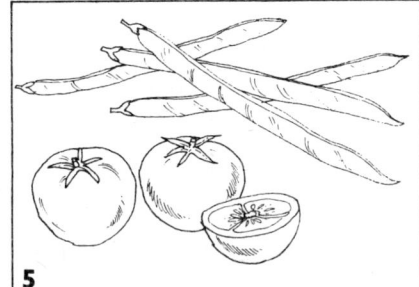

8 Take the order

Now listen to these guests. They are ordering vegetables. Write down the orders.

Holiday Inn

1 _____

2 _____

3 _____
_____
_____

4 _____
_____
_____

5 _____
_____
_____

6 _____
_____
_____

UNIT 6

1 Giving messages

Maria works in the Holiday Inn in Madrid. Sometimes guests ask her to give messages to people who come or telephone the restaurant. Look at the pictures and words below. Then give the people the messages, like this:

... Mr Barbero?

GUEST: Has Mr Barbero arrived yet?
MARIA: *He says he's arriving at 7.30.*

arrive/7.30

... Miss Linz?

1 wait/bar

... Mr Hussein?

2 expect/lounge

...Mrs Carmichael?

3 come/8 o'clock

...Miss Andreotti?

4 wait/verandah

... Mr Yamashta?

5 make/phone call

... Mrs Kim?

6 arrive/half an hour

1 Where can I find Miss Linz?

_____

2 Do you know where Mr Hussein is?

_____

3 What's happened to Mrs Carmichael?

_____

4 Is Miss Andreotti here?

_____

5 I was expecting to meet Mr Yamashta here.

_____

6 Has anything happened to Mrs Kim?

_____

2 More messages

Read the messages below.

Now give the message to the person who asks for it, like this:

1 _Hello, Mr Sanchez. Mr Li says he'll see you in the bar._

2 _____

_____

3 _____

_____

4 _____

_____

5 _____

_____

6 _____

_____

3 Saying you're sorry

Sometimes you have to apologise to people. Apologise to these people, like this:

My name's Laporte. I was expecting to meet Mr Smith this evening.
I'm terribly sorry, Mr Laporte. Mr Smith won't be able to meet you this evening.

1 My name's Robinson. I'm supposed to have lunch with Mrs Carmichael today.

_____

_____

2 My name's Mrs Chan. I'm having breakfast with Miss Nilsson this morning.

_____

_____

3 Do you know where Miss Henderson is? I was supposed to meet her before lunch.
My name's Jacques.

_____

_____

4 My name's Loewenthal. Mr Svensson is joining me for dinner this evening.

_____

_____

5 My name's Schmidt. I was hoping to meet Mrs Li for drinks.

_____

_____

_____

4 How do you help them?

Sometimes guests have problems. Look at what these guests say, then say what you will do to help them. Use these phrases:

tell the chef	fetch a clean one	*get some ice*	get the wine waiter
	bring you some		

GUEST: It's my whisky. It's warm.
YOU: *I'm very sorry, madam. I'll get some ice immediately.*

1 It's my knife. It's dirty.

_____

2 There's no bread.

_____

3 This fish is bad, you know. It tastes terrible.

_____

4 It's the wine. There's something wrong with it.

_____

5 The lunch menu

Read through the lunch menu below. Then turn on your cassette. Some guests are ordering lunch. Listen to their orders. Then read the answers in your book. Listen to the order again and put a tick ☑ against the right answer.

HORS D'OEUVRES

Duck terrine **Chicken liver pâté** **Soup of the day**	**Whitebait** **Fresh grapefuit** **Avocado vinaigrette**	**Prawn cocktail** **Smoked salmon** **Curry stuffed eggs**

SALADS

Ham **Roast beef** **Chicken**	**Tuna** **Lobster mayonnaise** **Californian salad**	**Mixed vegetable** **Egg mayonnaise** **Salade Niçoise**

FISH DISHES

Halibut **Trout with almonds**	**Salmon steak** **Tuna steak**	**Sole meunière** **Plaice**

MEAT DISHES

Boeuf stroganoff **Goulash** **Steak and mushroom** **pie**	**Roast lamb** **Mixed grill** **Veal escalope**	**Pork chops with orange** **Braised pork chops** **Gammon and apricot** **casserole**

SWEETS

From the trolley

---

1 The guest wants
   a smoked salmon. ☐
   b avocado vinaigrette. ☐
   c soup. ☐

2 The guest wants
   a roast beef. ☐
   b goulash. ☐
   c boeuf stroganoff. ☐

3 The guest wants
   a lobster mayonnaise. ☐
   b egg mayonnaise. ☐
   c Californian salad. ☐

4 The guest wants
   a gammon and apricot casserole. ☐
   b veal escalope. ☐
   c pork chops with orange. ☐

5 The guest wants
   a tuna steak. ☐
   b sole meunière. ☐
   c plaice. ☐

6 The guest wants
   a curry stuffed eggs. ☐
   b egg mayonnaise. ☐
   c lobster mayonnaise. ☐

7 The guest wants
   a roast lamb. ☐
   b veal escalope. ☐
   c steak and mushroom pie. ☐

8 The guest wants
   a pork chops with orange. ☐
   b mixed grill. ☐
   c braised pork chops. ☐

6 Some conversations

Here are some conversations. Listen to the conversations and follow them in your book. Then rewind your cassette. Start the conversation again. This time, speak to the guest at the same time as the voice on the cassette.

GUEST:	Good afternoon.
WAITER:	Good afternoon, madam. May I take your order?
GUEST:	Yes, please. I'll have the chicken liver pâté to start with.
WAITER:	Chicken liver pâté, madam. And what would you like to follow?
GUEST:	Tell me, how is the trout with almonds cooked?
WAITER:	It's fried in butter, madam, with blanched almonds. Then there's a squeeze of lemon juice.
GUEST:	That sounds fine. I'll have that.
WAITER:	And trout with almonds. Thank you, madam.

GUEST:	Good afternoon.
WAITRESS:	Good afternoon, sir. Are you ready to order?
GUEST:	I think so. I'll start with the curry stuffed eggs, and my friend will have the duck terrine.
WAITRESS:	One curry stuffed eggs, one duck terrine. And to follow, sir?
GUEST:	My friend will have the halibut.
WAITRESS:	The halibut, certainly, sir.
GUEST:	And what exactly is the boeuf stroganoff?
WAITRESS:	It's strips of steak, sir, fried in butter. It's cooked with onion and mushrooms, and a little seasoning. Then warm, soured cream is added.
GUEST:	It sounds very good. What are the vegetables?
WAITRESS:	Buttered rice, sir, or boiled potatoes if you prefer.
GUEST:	The rice, please.
WAITRESS:	Certainly, sir. That's one halibut and one boeuf stroganoff with rice.
GUEST:	That's it. Thank you.

GUEST 1:	Ah, good. Some lunch, please, I'm starving.
WAITER:	Certainly, sir. Have you decided what to have?
GUEST 1:	I think so. I'll certainly start with the soup of the day.
WAITER:	Soup to start with. And for the lady, sir?
GUEST 2:	I'll have the prawn cocktail.
WAITER:	Prawn cocktail. And to follow, madam?
GUEST 2:	The plaice. How is it done?
WAITER:	It's a fried fillet of plaice, madam. It's dipped in beaten egg, covered with breadcrumbs and then fried. It's served with a piece of lemon and tartare sauce.
GUEST 2:	I'll have that.
WAITER:	And for you, sir?
GUEST 1:	What comes in the mixed grill?
WAITER:	Pork sausages, sir. A lamb chop, bacon and kidney. It's garnished with tomatoes and mushrooms.
GUEST 1:	And chips?
WAITER:	Yes, sir.
GUEST 1:	That'll do me nicely.
WAITER:	Thank you, sir. That's one prawn cocktail and one soup, followed by one plaice and a mixed grill.
GUEST 1:	That's it.

7 Take the order

 Now listen to these guests. They are ordering meals. Look at the menu on page 38 and write down the orders.

Holiday Inn

1 _____

2 _____

3 _____

_____

_____

4 _____

_____

_____

5 _____

_____

_____

6 _____

_____

_____

_____

UNIT 7

1 Telling guests what to do

Look at these pictures and read the sentences. Then match the pictures with the correct sentence.

1 _____   2 _____   3 _____

4 _____   5 _____   6 _____

a Excuse me, gentlemen. I must ask you to leave. We're closing now.
b Excuse me, madam. You must go immediately. That's the fire alarm.
c Excuse me, sir. You mustn't sit there. It's reserved.
d Excuse me, madam. You mustn't smoke here. It's a no smoking area.
e Excuse me, ladies. You mustn't make so much noise. It's annoying the other guests.
f Excuse me, madam. You mustn't leave your coat there. Someone may steal it.

2 When you can't help

Sometimes you can't help a guest yourself. But you can tell them what they must do. Look at what these guests say and tell them what to do.

I'm	sorry afraid	I can't help you,	sir. madam.	You'll have to	go wait speak ring deposit	to the travel agent. them at reception. to the post office. until a table is free. to the manager. his room.

41

1 But I want a table now. Not in half an hour's time.

_____

_____

2 Can you put my valuables in a safe place, please?

_____

_____

3 Do you know where Mr Sanchez is?

_____

_____

4 Are there any nice trips we could make over the weekend?

_____

_____

5 Can you get me some stamps for these letters, please?

_____

_____

6 I'm afraid I've lost my wallet, so I can't pay. What do you suggest I do?

_____

_____

3 Helping the guest

Look at what these guests say. Then use the sentences below to help the guest, like this:

GUEST: Where is Miss Sneddon, do you know?
YOU: _If you like, I'll ring her room for you, madam._

If you ask at reception,	I'll take your order, sir.
If you like,	I'll bring your drinks to you, sir.
If you're uncomfortable,	they'll be able to help you, sir.
If you take a seat,	I'll get the chef, sir.
If you're ready,	I'll find you another table, sir.

1 Do you know which room Mr Singh is in?

_____

2 That was a terrible meal.

_____

3 It's very hot here, you know.

_____

4 I can't carry all these drinks, you know.

_____

5 Ah, waiter, good.

_____

4 Passing messages

Look at the messages these guests ask you to give to other people. Then pass the message, like this:

YOU: *He said he would be late, sir.*

1 _____

2 _____

3 _____

4 _____

5 _____

6 _____

5 The dinner menu

Read through the dinner menu below. Then turn on your cassette. Some guests are ordering dinner. Listen to their orders. Then read the answers in your book. Listen to the order again and put a tick ☑ against the right answer.

APPETIZERS	Consommé Mixed vegetable soup Avacado with prawns	Pâté maison Liver terrine Melon	Sardines stuffed with spinach Smoked salmon Taramasalata[1]
FISH DISHES	Grilled sea bass with herbs Turbot with crab sauce	Fish kebabs Baked halibut	Deep fried scampi Baked red mullet
MEAT DISHES	Spaghetti Bolognese Rump steak fines herbes[2] Spanish pork with olives	Roast turkey Beef with green peppers Italian veal casserole	Spare ribs Chicken fricassée Coq au vin[3]
SWEETS	Peach Melba Fresh fruit salad	Chocolate rum gateau Lemon sorbet	Crême caramel Apple strudel[4]
WINES	**White** Entre-deux-Mers Meursault Bernkasteler Niersteiner	**Rosé** Rosé d'Anjou Rosé de Provence	**Red** Beaujolais Chianti Rioja Côtes du Rhône

NOTES: [1]Taramasalata is a Greek appetizer. It is made with smoked cod's roe, olive oil, garlic and lemon juice. [2]Fines herbes means with chopped herbs. [3]Chicken pieces cooked in a red wine sauce with bacon, onions and mushroom. [4]Apple strudel: a kind of apple pastry.

1 The guest wants
  a taramasalata. ☐
  b melon. ☐
  c sardines. ☐

2 The guest wants
  a mullet. ☐
  b turbot. ☐
  c halibut. ☐

3 The guest wants
  a bass. ☐
  b turbot. ☐
  c fish kebabs. ☐

4 The guest wants
  a veal casserole. ☐
  b coq au vin. ☐
  c roast turkey. ☐

5 The guest wants
  a chicken fricassée. ☐
  b spare ribs. ☐
  c beef with green peppers. ☐

6 The guest wants
  a crême caramel. ☐
  b apple strudel. ☐
  c fruit salad. ☐

7 The guest wants
  a Meursault. ☐
  b Bernkasteler. ☐
  c Niersteiner. ☐

8 The guest wants
  a Rosé de Provence. ☐
  b Chianti. ☐
  c Beaujolais. ☐

6 Some conversations

Here are some conversations. Listen to the conversations and follow them in your book. Then rewind your cassette. Start the conversation again. This time, speak to the guest at the same time as the voice on the cassette.

GUEST: Ah, good evening.
WAITRESS: Good evening, madam. What would you like tonight?
GUEST: What's taramasalata?
WAITRESS: It's a Greek dish, madam. It's a kind of fish pâté, made with roe, olive oil, garlic and lemon juice.
GUEST: I'll try it.
WAITRESS: And what would you like to follow, madam?
GUEST: The scampi, please.
WAITRESS: And scampi. Would you like any wine this evening?
GUEST: Do you have half a bottle of Meursault?
WAITRESS: Not of Meursault, madam, no. But we do have half a bottle of the Entre-deux-Mers.
GUEST: I'll have that, then.
WAITRESS: Thank you, madam.

GUEST: That was very nice, thank you.
WAITER: Would you like a sweet, madam?
GUEST: Yes, but nothing too filling. What do you suggest?
WAITER: An ice, perhaps? The lemon sorbet, for instance?
GUEST: No, not that. I'll have the crême caramel.
WAITER: Crême caramel. And would you like coffee afterwards?
GUEST: Yes, please.
WAITER: Thank you, madam.

GUEST: I'll have the pâté maison, please, and my friend will have the smoked salmon.
WAITER: One pâté, one smoked salmon, sir.
GUEST: And then the mullet . . . and, er . . .
WAITER: One mullet, sir.
GUEST: Well, I'd like fish too. But not mullet. What do you recommend?
WAITER: The turbot's very good, sir. The crab sauce is excellent. It's one of our chef's specialities.
GUEST: I'll try that, then. Now, wine. A rosé. A Rosé de Provence, I think.
WAITER: And a bottle of Rosé de Provence. Thank you, sir.

GUEST 1: Would you like a sweet, Mr Kleist?
GUEST 2: I'll have the gâteau, thanks.
WAITRESS: A gâteau. And for you, madam?
GUEST 1: The apple strudel, please.
WAITRESS: And a strudel. Would you like coffee afterwards?
GUEST 1: What about you, Mr Kleist?
GUEST 2: Yes, please. And a brandy, if I may.
GUEST 1: Just coffee for me.
WAITRESS: Two coffees, madam, and a brandy.
GUEST 1: That's it, thank you.

Now listen to these guests. They are ordering meals. Look at the menu on page 44 and write down the orders.

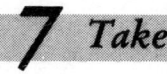

Holiday Inn

1 _____

2 _____

3 _____
_____
_____

4 _____
_____
_____

5 _____
_____
_____

6 _____
_____
_____

UNIT 8

1 Making requests

Look at these pictures and read the sentences. Then match the pictures with the sentences.

1 _____   2 _____   3 _____

4 _____   5 _____   6 _____

a Would you mind coming with me, madam? I'll take you to the manager.
b Would you mind waiting five minutes, sir? We're full at the moment.
c Would you mind making less noise, gentlemen? You're disturbing the other guests.
d Would you mind waiting a moment, sir? I'm serving this lady.
e Would you mind moving, madam? This table is reserved.
f Would you mind sitting here, madam? All the other tables are occupied.

2 When do you start?

Look at the notice below. It tells you when your restaurant, cafeteria and bar open and close.

RESTAURANT		CAFETERIA
Breakfast		**Open**
07.00 – 10.00		*09.00 – 18.00*
Lunch		
12.00 – 14.00		**BAR**
Dinner		**Open**
19.00 – 22.00		*10.00 – 15.00*
		17.00 – 02.00

Now answer the guests' questions. Use the words *start* and *stop*, like this:

1 When does lunch begin?
We start serving at 12.00, sir/madam.
_____

2 When does the bar close? At night?
_____
_____

3 How early can I get breakfast?
_____
_____

4 When does the restaurant shut? For dinner?
_____
_____

5 How long does the cafeteria stay open?
_____
_____

6 When does the bar open in the mornings?
_____
_____

7 How soon can we get dinner?
_____
_____

8 When does breakfast finish?
_____
_____

3 *What do you say?*

Something is wrong with the guest's table. Say what you will have/get done about it, like this:

This table's filthy. Look at it!
clean
I'll have/get it cleaned immediately, sir/madam.
_____

1 This tablecloth's dirty.
change
_____
_____

2 This wine tastes off to me.
replace
_____
_____

3 Those men are annoying my wife. Can you do something?
move
_____
_____

4 We've been waiting ten minutes for our aperitifs.
bring
_____
_____

5 We're in a hurry. Can we have lunch now, please?
serve
_____
_____

4 *What's wrong?*

Look at these pictures and the words below them. Then say what needs doing, like this:

flowers/arrange
The flowers need arranging.

1 tablecloth/wash

2 tables/clear

3 glass/replace

4 cutlery/arrange

4 counter/wipe

6 floor/sweep

1 _____

2 _____

3 _____

4 _____

5 _____

6 _____

5 *The menu*

Read through the menu below. Then turn on your cassette. Some guests are ordering dinner. Listen to their orders. Then read the answers in your book. Listen to the order again and put a tick ☑ against the right answer.

APERITIFS

Whiskey	Sherry	Campari	Dubonnet
Bourbon	Wine by the glass	Pastis	Cinzano
Gin	Vodka	Perrier	Rum

STARTERS

Salade Niçoise	Herring salad
Mussels à la Marinière	Soup of the day
Oysters (1/2 dozen)	Chicken liver pâté
Antipasto[1]	Mushroom in
Stuffed squid	garlic butter

VEGETABLES

Cabbage	Cauliflower
Peas	Leeks
Broad beans	Mushrooms
Runner beans	Tomatoes
Spincach	Chips
Brussels sprouts	Roast potatoes
Onions	Boiled potatoes
Broccoli	

FISH

Grilled sea bass	Deep fried
with herbs	scampi
Grilled sole	Baked scallops
Lobster Thermidor	Tuna steak

MEAT

Tournedos Rossini[2]	Boeuf à la
Entrecôte[2]	Bourguignonne[3]
Lamb kebabs	Rabbit stewed in
Roast venison	red wine
Veal escalope	Duck with
Beef curry	orange sauce

NOTES: [1] An Italian dish made of cold meats and salad vegetables. [2] Two different kinds of steak. [3] A French beef stew.

1 The guest wants
  a a glass of white wine. ☐
  b a glass of red wine. ☐
  c a glass of rosé wine. ☐

2 The guest wants
  a a neat whisky. ☐
  b a whisky with ice. ☐
  c a whisky with water. ☐

3 The guest wants
  a oysters and venison. ☐
  b mussels and duck. ☐
  c oysters and duck. ☐

4 The guest wants
  a scallops with mushrooms. ☐
  b mushrooms and then scallops. ☐
  c mussels and scallops. ☐

5 The guest wants
  a soup and scampi. ☐
  b soup and scallops. ☐
  c Salade Niçoise and scampi. ☐

6 The guest wants his tournedos
  a well done. ☐
  b medium. ☐
  c rare. ☐

7 The guest wants entrecôte with
  a peas and tomatoes. ☐
  b beans, mushrooms and
    tomatoes. ☐
  c peas, mushrooms and
    tomatoes. ☐

8 The guest wants
  a Salade Niçoise and venison. ☐
  b herring salad and venison. ☐
  c herring salad and veal escalope. ☐

6 Some conversations

Here are some conversations. Listen to the conversations and follow them in your book. Then rewind your cassette. Start the conversation again. This time, speak to the guest at the same time as the voice on the cassette.

GUEST 1:   Yes, we're ready to order, thank you. My wife'll start with the mussels.
WAITER: Mussels, yes, sir. And for you?
GUEST 1:   What is this antipasto?
WAITER: It's an Italian starter, sir. It's a variety of cold meats, like salami, and a little tuna. And salad vegetables, lettuce, tomato, cucumber and so on. It's quite filling.
GUEST 1:   It sounds very good. I'll try that.
WAITER: One antipasto. And what would you like to follow, madam?
GUEST 2:   I'll have the sole, please.
WAITER: What vegetables would you like with your sole, madam?
GUEST 2:   None, I think. Just some lemon.
WAITER: No vegetables. And for you, sir?
GUEST 1:   I'll have the entrecôte, please.
WAITER: How would you like it done, sir?
GUEST 1:   Medium rare.
WAITER: Medium rare. And vegetables?
GUEST 1:   Mushrooms, chips and, er, yes, peas.
WAITER: Mushrooms, chips and peas. Thank you, sir.

GUEST 1:   To start with, we'll have a gin and tonic and a Perrier water.
WAITRESS: One Perrier water and a gin and tonic, madam.
GUEST 1:   And then we'll have a herring salad . . .
WAITRESS: One herring salad . . .
GUEST 2:   And the mushrooms in garlic butter for me.
WAITRESS: And to follow, madam?
GUEST 1:   What was it, Peter? The rabbit?
GUEST 2:   Yes, rabbit, please.
WAITRESS: One rabbit.
GUEST 1:   And veal escalope for me.
WAITRESS: That's one herring salad, one mushrooms, one rabbit and an escalope, with a Perrier water and a gin and tonic to start with.
GUEST 1:   That's right. And thanks.

GUEST 1:   Ah, and about time, too. We'll have a bourbon, and, and, er . . . what do you call it over here? Whisky? OK, one whisky . . . Hey, do you want ice? No? I guess that's one whisky, whatever . . .
WAITRESS: Yes, sir. One bourbon, one whisky.
GUEST 1:   Then, say, are these oysters clean over here, eh? I mean, are they?
WAITRESS: Yes, sir.
GUEST 1:   OK, oysters. And a tournedos. Well done. What about you, Rob?
GUEST 2:   The squid, and then the venison, please, miss.
WAITRESS: That's a whisky and a bourbon, then one oysters, one squid, followed by a tournedos, well done, and the venison.
GUEST 1:   That's it.

Now listen to these guests. They are ordering meals. Look at the menu on page 50 and write down the orders.

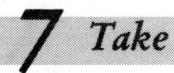

1 _____

2 _____

3 _____

4 _____

5 _____

6 _____

UNIT 9

1 Giving advice

Look at these pictures and read the sentences. Then match the pictures with the sentences.

1 _____ 2 _____ 3 _____

4 _____ 5 _____ 6 _____

a If I were you, I'd try the oysters. They're excellent at this time of year.
b If I were you, I'd have the prawn cocktail. It's very light.
c If I were you, I'd try the chicken. It's one of the chef's specialities.
d If I were you, I'd have the mushrooms. It's a local dish.
e If I were you, I'd have the grilled sole. It's caught locally.
f If I were you, I'd try the tournedos. It's very filling.

2 Polite requests

Look at what these guests say. Then choose the best answer from the table below.

	follow me,	I'll send the wine waiter.
	know the recipe,	you'll find it on your left.
	see the manager,	I'll take it to the cloakroom.
If you'd like to	sit down,	I'll see if we have one free.
	wait a moment,	I'll show you to his table.
	give it to me,	I'll see if she's available.
	have some advice on wine,	I'll ask the chef.
	go up to the first floor,	I'll bring your drinks to you.

1 I can't carry all these drinks. Have you got a tray?

_____

_____

2 Where can I put my coat?

_____

_____

3 Where is Mr Aziz sitting?

_____

_____

4 Where's the night club?

_____

_____

5 What's in this sauce? It's excellent.

_____

_____

6 I really don't know which wine to choose.

_____

_____

7 I want to make a complaint. Who's in charge here?

_____

_____

8 Have you got a free table?

_____

_____

3 Answering questions

Look at these guests' questions. Then answer their questions, like this:

When does the cafeteria shut?
half an hour
It will/It'll be shutting in half an hour, madam.

1 When does the restaurant open?
ten minutes

_____

2 When does the bar close?
an hour

_____

3 When's my aperitif coming?
a moment

_____

4 When are our steaks coming?
two or three minutes

_____

5 When is Mr Hussein arriving?
8 o'clock

_____

4 Asking questions

Look at what these guests say. Then ask them a question, like this:

Can I make a reservation?
When/arrive?
Certainly, sir. When will you be arriving?

I I'll have some extra guests for dinner.
How many/bring?

_____

2 Tell Mr Jones I'll wait for him.
Where/wait?

_____

3 I'd like to settle the bill, please.
How/pay?

_____

4 I'd like to wait for my wife.
When/come?

_____

5 Can you show Mr Aziz to my table when he comes?
Where/sit?

_____

5 A menu

Read through the menu on the next page. Then turn on your cassette. Some guests are ordering lunch. Listen to their orders. Then read the answers in your book. Listen to the order again and put a tick ☑ against the right answer.

I The guest wants
  a a mineral water.   ☐
  b a beer.   ☐
  c a tomato juice.   ☐

2 The guest wants
  a a dry sherry.   ☐
  b a sweet sherry.   ☐
  c a medium sherry.   ☐

3 The guest wants
  a curried prawns.   ☐
  b a prawn cocktail.   ☐
  c king prawns.   ☐

4 The guest wants
  a pike mousse.   ☐
  b pâté maison.   ☐
  c mussels.   ☐

5 The guest wants
  a moussaka.   ☐
  b mullet.   ☐
  c hare in cream sauce.   ☐

6 The guest wants
  a chicken chasseur   ☐
  b coq au vin.   ☐
  c roast duck.   ☐

7 The guest wants
  a spare ribs. ☐
  b Spanish pork. ☐
  c sole. ☐

8 The guest wants
  a goulash. ☐
  b entrecôte. ☐
  c veal casserole. ☐

APERITIFS

Cocktails to choice	Campari
Fruit juices to choice	Dubonnet
Gin	Cinzano
Whisky	Vodka
Sherry	Pastis
Vodka	Rum

HORS D'OEUVRES

Shellfish cocktail	Mussels à
Curried prawns	la Marinière
King prawns[1]	Pâté maison
Clams	Melon
Pike mousse	Consommé

MAIN DISHES

Turbot with crab sauce
Stuffed fillets of sole
Baked red mullet
Moussaka[2]
Hare in cream sauce
Italian veal casserole
Spare ribs
Spanish pork with olives
Veal escalope
Boeuf à la Bourgignonne
Entrecôte
Roast duck
Coq au vin
Chicken Chasseur
Goulash

SWEETS

From the trolley

NOTES: [1]King here means 'very big'. [2]Moussaka: a Greek dish, mainly minced beef and aubergines.

6 Some conversations

Here are some conversations. Listen to the conversations and follow them in your book. Then rewind your cassette. Listen to the conversation again. This time, speak to the guest at the same time as the voice on the cassette.

GUEST: My wife'll have a Dubonnet to start with, and I'll have a mineral water, if you've got one.
WAITRESS: Yes, sir, we have Perrier or a Scottish mineral water called Highland Spring.
GUEST: I'll have the Highland Spring.
WAITRESS: Certainly, sir. And a Dubonnet. And will you be having a starter?
GUEST: Sure. The curried prawns and the clams, please.
WAITRESS: One curried prawns, one clams.
GUEST: And after that I'll have the hare, and my wife would like the coq au vin.
WAITRESS: And a hare and a coq au vin. Thank you, sir.

WAITER: Good afternoon, madam. Have you chosen yet?
GUEST: Yes. The mussels to start with for me. And my friend will have the mousse. The pike mousse.
WAITER: Mussels and a pike mousse. What would you like to follow, madam?

GUEST: I'm afraid we can't really make up our minds. Is there anything you particularly recommend?

WAITER: Well, madam, if I were you, I'd try the hare in cream sauce. It's one of our chef's local specialities. It's really excellent.

GUEST: OK, we'll try that. Two, please.

WAITER: Thank you, madam.

WAITRESS: Good afternoon, gentlemen. Are you ready to order?

GUEST 1:   Sure am. What about you, Bill? A drink to start with?

GUEST 2:   A double whisky on the rocks for me.

GUEST 1:   Make that two.

WAITRESS: Two whiskies with ice, yes, sir.

GUEST 1:   Then I'll have the shellfish cocktail.

GUEST 2:   And I'll have the curried prawns. Not too hot, are they?

WAITRESS: No, sir. Quite mild, really.

GUEST 2:   OK, then.

WAITRESS: The shellfish cocktail for you sir, and one curried prawns. And what would you like after that?

GUEST 1:   Moussaka for me.

WAITRESS: One moussaka. And for you, sir?

GUEST 2:   I'll have the entrecôte.

WAITRESS: Certainly, sir. How would you like it done?

GUEST 2:   Medium rare, please.

WAITRESS: One entrecôte, medium rare. Have you chosen a wine yet?

GUEST 1:   I guess I forgot about that. Can you come back in a moment or two?

WAITRESS: Of course, sir. I'll fetch your aperitifs.

GUEST 1:   Thanks.

7 Take the order

Now listen to these guests. They are ordering meals. Look at the menu on page 56 and write down the orders.

Holiday Inn

1 _____

_____

2 _____

_____

3 _____

_____

_____

4 _____

_____

_____

5 _____

_____

_____

6 _____

_____

_____

_____

UNIT 10

In this last Unit, practise what you have learnt!

1 *The breakfast order*

Look at the breakfast menu below. Then turn on your cassette and write down the guests' orders.

BREAKFAST

Two fresh eggs, any style
Fried, poached, scrambled boiled

Omelettes
Plain, tomato, ham, cheese, bacon, mushroom

Vegetable salad

Fruit juice
Tomato, apple, grapefruit, orange

Croissant
Toast
Danish pastry
Toasted wheatgerm bread
Yoghurt
Plain, fruit
Oatmeal

Coffee, caffeine free coffee
Tea, chocolate, milk

Holiday Inn

1 _____

2 _____

3 _____

4 _____

5 _____

Look at these pictures and read the sentences. Then match the pictures with the sentences.

1 _____   2 _____   3 _____

4 _____   5 _____   6 _____

a If I were you, I'd have the oysters. They're in season.
b Would you mind waiting a moment, sir? We're full.
c I'll take it away, madam.
d Excuse me, madam. You mustn't smoke here. It's a no smoking area.
e If you'd like to follow me, I'll show you to your table.
f May I take your order, madam?

First look through the bar list below. Then turn on your cassette. Some guests are ordering drinks. Write down the orders on the next page.

BAR LIST

WHISKY
Scotch Proprietary
Scotch Regular
Irish
Rye
Bourbon
Malt & Deluxe

GIN
Proprietary
Regular

VODKA
Proprietary
Regular
Stolichnaya

RUM
Commodore
Bacardi

COGNAC (1/6 Gill)
Louis Bernard
Martell 3 Star
Remy Martin 3 Star
Remy Martin VSOP

ARMAGNAC (1/6 Gill)
Janneau 1961

LIQUEURS

MIXERS & MINERALS
Baby Mixers
Baby Juices
Coke
Perrier 220 ml
Splits

APERITIFS
Willoughbys Special No. 20 Port
Grahams White Port
Warres 1975 Vintage Port
Willoughbys Sherries
Tio Pepe
Croft Original
Bristol Cream
Campari
Pernod/Ricard

VERMOUTHS
Dubonnet
Martini/Cinzano

WINE
House per Glass

CHAMPAGNE
House per Glass

*GIN, WHISKY, VODKA, RUM ARE SERVED
IN MEASURES OF 1/3 GILL
OR MULTIPLES THEREOF*

1 _____

2 _____

3 _____

_____

_____

4 _____

_____

_____

5 _____

_____

_____

6 _____

_____

_____

_____

Read through the menu below. Then turn on your cassette. Some guests are ordering meals. Write down the guests' orders on the next page.

☆☆☆☆☆☆☆☆ HORS D'OEUVRES ☆☆☆☆☆☆☆☆

Consommé	Mushrooms in garlic	Pâté maison
Soup of the day	Mussels à la marinière	Duck terrine
Melon with Parma ham	Pike mousse	Eggs mayonnaise
Prawn cocktail	Curried prawns	Antipasto

☆☆☆☆☆☆☆☆☆ FISH DISHES ☆☆☆☆☆☆☆☆☆

Lobster thermidor	Baked red mullet	Grilled sea bass
Grilled sole	Baked scallops	Deep fried scampi
Stuffed fillets of sole	Tuna steak	Turbot with crab sauce

☆☆☆☆☆☆☆☆☆ MEAT DISHES ☆☆☆☆☆☆☆☆☆

Tournedos Rossini	Coq au vin	Veal casserole
Entrecôte	Roast chicken	Veal escalope
Rump steak	Roast duck	Hare in cream sauce
Boeuf à la Bourguignonne	Spare ribs	Rabbit stewed in red wine
Goulash	Spanish pork with olives	Mixed grill

☆☆☆☆☆☆☆☆☆☆ SALADS ☆☆☆☆☆☆☆☆☆☆

Salad Niçoise	Beef	Tuna
Chicken	Hawaiian,	Mixed vegetable
Ham	Californian	Egg
Turkey		

☆☆☆☆☆☆☆☆☆ VEGETABLES ☆☆☆☆☆☆☆☆☆

Cabbage	Onions	Mushrooms
Peas	Brussels sprouts	Tomatoes
Broad beans	Broccoli	French fries
Runner beans	Cauliflower	Potatoes
Spinach	Leeks	(roast, boiled)

☆☆☆☆☆☆☆☆☆ SWEETS ☆☆☆☆☆☆☆☆☆

Apple strudel	Lemon sorbet	Black Forest gâteau
Peach Melba	Crème caramel	Fresh fruit salad

1 _____

2 _____

3 _____

4 _____

5 _____

6 _____

KEY TO EXERCISES

Unit 1

1 WHAT DO THEY DO?

2 She's a waitress.
3 She's a receptionist.
4 He's a porter.
5 She's a cashier.
6 He's a barman.
7 She's a maid.
8 He's a head waiter.
10 The waitress works in the restaurant. She serves the meals.
11 The receptionist works at the front desk. She welcomes the guests.
12 The porter works all over the hotel. He carries the luggage.
13 The cashier works at the front desk. She prepares the bills.
14 The barman works in the bar. He serves the drinks.
15 The maid works in the bedrooms. She cleans them.
16 The head waiter works in the restaurant. He supervises the waiters.

2 IN THE RESTAURANT

1 Each place has got a soup spoon. There's a soup spoon for each place.
2 Each place has got three knives. There are three knives for each place.
3 It's got a tablecloth. There's a tablecloth on the table.
4 It's got an ashtray. There's an ashtray on the table.
5 Each place has got two wine glasses. There are two wine glasses for each place.
6 Each place has got a napkin. There's a napkin for each place.
7 It's got a menu. There's a menu on the table.
8 Each place has got a side plate. There's a side plate for each place.
9 It's got a wine list. There's a wine list on the table.
10 It's got a salt cellar. There's a salt cellar on the table.
11 The places haven't got any napkins. There aren't any napkins.
12 The places haven't got any forks. There aren't any forks.
13 The places haven't got any soup spoons. There aren't any soup spoons.
14 The places haven't got any wine glasses. There aren't any wine glasses.
15 The places haven't got any side plates. There aren't any side plates.
16 It (The table) hasn't got a salt cellar. There isn't a salt cellar.

3 WHAT DO YOU SAY?

2 f **3** a **4** c **5** d **6** b

4 TELL THE GUEST THE WAY

1 Certainly, madam. Turn *right* out of the restaurant. Go past the bar and the lounge is on your *left*.
2 *Certainly*, madam. Go across the foyer and *out of* the main entrance. Cross the street, go *past* the travel agent and the bank is *on your right*.
3 Certainly, sir. *Turn right out of* the restaurant. Go *past* the hairdresser and the night club is *on your right*.
4 *Certainly*, sir. Go *across* the foyer and out of the *main entrance*. *Cross* the street and the disco is *on your left*.
5 Certainly, madam. *Go out of* the restaurant. *Cross* the foyer and the *boutique* is on your right.

5 WHAT DOES THE GUEST WANT?

Tapescript
Peter works in the Holiday Inn, Manchester. Guests order food and drinks from him.

65

Listen to the guests' orders. Then read the answers in your book. Listen to the question again, and put a tick against the right answer. Here's number one.

GUEST: Is that room service?
PETER: Yes, sir, it is.
GUEST: I'd like a bottle of white wine, please. It's room twenty-one.
PETER: Certainly, sir.

Number 2
GUEST: Good evening. I'd like a whisky, please with ice.
PETER: Certainly, sir.

Number 3
GUEST: What shall I start with? Well, not the melon. Not the salad. I know, I'll have the soup.
PETER: Thank you, madam.

Number 4
GUEST: Then, let me see. I'm not very hungry, so not the steak. I'll have the fish. I prefer that to an omelette.
PETER: Thank you, madam.

Number 5
GUEST: I'd like an aperitif before dinner. I'll have a gin and tonic, please, with half a bottle of rosé wine with the meal. Red wine's too heavy for me.
PETER: Thank you, sir.

Key
1 c 2 c 3 b 4 b 5 a

7 OFFERING FOOD AND DRINK

You will now hear some guests. Choose the sentence which answers the guest. Say the sentence onto the cassette. You will then hear the right answer. Are you ready? Here's the first guest.

GUEST: I want something hot to start with.
YOU: Would you like the soup, madam?

Number 2
GUEST: I like fish as a starter.
YOU: Would you like the smoked salmon, madam?

Number 3
GUEST: Can you recommend a German white wine?
YOU: Would you like the Baden dry, sir, or perhaps the Piesporter?

Number 4
GUEST: I want something light as a main course.
YOU: Would you like a salad, sir?

Number 5
GUEST: Can you suggest a French white wine?
YOU: Would you like the Bordeaux Blanc de Blancs, madam, or perhaps the Chablis?

Number 6
GUEST: Have you got a rosé wine?
YOU: Would you like the Anjou Rosé, madam?

Number 7
GUEST: I've got a large appetite. I want something really filling as a main course.
YOU: Would you like the fillet steak, sir?

Number 8
GUEST: Have you got something with eggs? That's what I'd really like.
YOU: Would you like the omelette, madam?

Now listen to these guests. They are ordering their meals. Look at the menu on page 6 and write down the orders.

Number 1
GUEST: I think I'll have the prawn cocktail to start with, please, and then the beef salad.

Number 2
GUEST: My wife will have the sole, please, and I'll have the lamb cutlets. And we'd also like a bottle of Anjou Rosé.

Number 3
GUEST: It's one soup, and two smoked salmons. And then one fillet steak, one chicken Kiev and a sole. Also, we'll have a bottle of the Chablis, please.

Number 4
GUEST: Two Salades Niçoises, one melon and smoked salmon to begin with. And then—what was it?—Oh yes, one omelette, one lamb cutlets, one chicken salad and a ham salad. And we'll have a bottle of the Niersteiner Domtal and one of the Côtes du Rhône. That's all, thanks.

Number 5
GUEST: I'll take the pâté to start with, and my husband wants the smoked salmon. He'll have the fillet steak after that, and I'll have the chicken salad. And a bottle of Franken Sylvaner to go with it.

Number 6
GUEST: Three melons and a pâté, followed by one lamb cutlets and three soles. And we'll have the Goldener Oktober to start with, and then the Mouton Cadet to follow. OK? Thanks.

Key
For the key, look at the tapescript above.

Unit 2

1 WHAT DO YOU SAY?

1 f **2** b **3** e **4** c **5** d **6** a

2 ASKING QUESTIONS

1 Where **2** How **3** When **4** What **5** What **6** Who **7** How **8** How **9** What **10** Where

3 ANSWERING QUESTIONS

1 It costs eighteen marks.
2 It closes at two in the morning.
3 We don't charge for service.
4 They open at 9.30.
5 We sell cigarettes in the foyer.
6 We don't allow pets in the restaurant.
7 We accept most credit cards.
8 We serve light meals in the cafeteria.
9 We offer set menus as well.
10 We buy all our vegetables fresh.

4 ANSWER THE GUESTS' QUESTIONS

2 closed **3** asked **4** put **5** waited; left **6** reserved **7** took; thought **8** ordered

5 ASKING THE GUEST QUESTIONS

2 I'm sorry, madam. What *did you order*?
3 What *did you leave* on the table, sir?

4 I see, sir. How *did you pay* it?

5 Who *did you speak* to, madam?

6 SAYING *NO* POLITELY

2 No, madam, I'm sorry. I'm afraid we didn't find it.

3 No, sir/madam, I'm sorry. I'm afraid we didn't know (that).

4 No, madam, I'm sorry. I'm afraid he/she didn't give it to us.

5 No, sir/madam, I'm sorry. I'm afraid he/she didn't ring us.

7 IN THE BAR

Tapescript

Some guests are ordering drinks. Listen to their orders. Then read the answers below. Listen to the order again, and put a tick against the right answer. Here's the first order.

GUEST: I'd like a vermouth, please, a Cinzano.

Number 2

GUEST 2:   Now, let's see, what shall I have. I know, a gin, please, regular, with tonic.

Number 3

GUEST 3:   I think I'll have a vodka. A Stolichnaya, please.

Number 4

GUEST 4:   I rather fancy a whisky, a rye whisky. OK?

Number 5

GUEST 5:   I don't want anything alcoholic. I'll take a Perrier water. With ice and lemon.

Number 6

GUEST 6:   For me, a brandy. Hm, not the Martell, and not the Remy Martin three star. Make it the Remy Martin VSOP, would you?

Number 7

GUEST 7:   A sherry for me, I don't like cream sherry very much, so that leaves a Tio Pepe or a Croft Original. The Tio Pepe, I think.

Number 8

GUEST 8:   I take it you have red, rosé and white house wines by the glass?

BARMAN: Yes, sir.

GUEST 8:   Red's too heavy, rosé I don't really go for. The white, please.

Key

1 c   **2** b   **3** c   **4** a   **5** c   **6** c   **7** b   **8** c

9 OFFERING DRINKS

You will now hear some guests. Choose the sentence which answers the guest. Say the sentence onto the cassette. You will then hear the right answer. Here's the first guest.

GUEST: I'd like a vermouth, please.

YOU: Would you like a Cinzano or a Martini, madam?

Number 2

GUEST: A whisky, please.

YOU: Would you like bourbon, rye or malt, sir?

Number 3

GUEST: Some kind of aperitif is what I'd like.

YOU: Would you like a Pernod or a sherry, sir?

Number 4

GUEST: I could do with a brandy.

YOU: Would you like a Louis Bernard, a Martell or a Remy Martin, madam?

Number 5

GUEST: I want something soft. What have you got?

YOU: Would you like a juice or a mineral water, madam?

Number 6

GUEST: A sherry, please.

YOU: Would you like a Tio Pepe, a Croft Original or a Bristol Cream, sir?

 10 TAKE THE ORDER

Now listen to these guests. They are ordering drinks. Look at the bar list and write down the orders.

Number 1

GUEST: I'll have a Graham's white port, please.

Number 2

GUEST: We'd like two armagnacs and a rye whisky, please.

Number 3

GUEST: Can you give us five glasses of champagne, please. Oh, and two glasses of white wine.

Number 4

GUEST: Now, let me see. That's one malt whisky for you, John, isn't it? Then a Perrier water, with ice and lemon. Now, what was yours, Anders? Oh, yes, a rum, a Bacardi. Two glasses of red wine and, for me, a Ricard.

Number 5

GUEST: A tomato juice, a Dubonnet, an Irish whisky and two Cinzanos, please.

Number 6

GUEST: A vodka and orange for me, please. What about you, Anne?

ANNE: A Tio Pepe, if that's all right.

GUEST: One Tio Pepe. No, make that two, please. And then a Coke for my daughter. And two glasses of rosé wine.

Key

For the key, look at the tapescript above.

Unit 3

1 ASKING QUESTIONS

1 c 2 f 3 a 4 e 5 d 6 b

2 SOME MORE QUESTIONS

1 Have you lost your wallet, sir?
2 Have you booked a table, sir/madam?
3 Have you chosen the wine, sir/madam?
4 Has your guest come, sir/madam?
5 Has your son finished, sir/madam?
6 Has your daughter had enough, sir/madam?

3 WHAT'S THE BEST ANSWER?

1 I've reserved a table by the window, madam.
2 I've put you in the corner, sir.
3 I've left a message in reception, madam.
4 I've arranged for them to play it at 9, sir.
5 I've ordered a special meal for him, madam.
6 I've told the barman to charge everything to you, sir.

4 SOME SHORT ANSWERS

1 No, sir/madam, I'm afraid I haven't.
2 No, sir/madam, I'm afraid they haven't.
3 No, sir/madam, I'm afraid she hasn't.
4 No, sir/madam, I'm afraid it hasn't.
5 No, sir, I'm afraid I/we haven't.

5 HE MAY HAVE GONE TO RECEPTION

1 I don't know, sir/madam. He may/could have gone to the bar.
2 I don't know, sir/madam. He may/could have cancelled his reservation.
3 I don't know, sir/madam. She may/could have eaten in her room.
4 I don't know, sir/madam. He may/could have decided to go outside.
5 I don't know, sir/madam. My colleague may/could have taken it to the cloakroom.
6 I don't know, sir/madam. He may/could have left early.

6 TALKING TO GUESTS

1 anywhere **2** nothing **3** Someone/Somebody **4** no one/nobody
5 somewhere **6** something **7** nowhere **8** anything **9** anyone

7 ROOM SERVICE

Tapescript

Some guests are ordering food. Listen to their orders. Then read the answers in your book. Listen to the order again and put a tick against the right order.

Number 1

I'd like a bowl of soup, please, the consommé. In room 462.

Number 2

Could you send two French onion soups to room 201, please?

Number 3

This is room 23. Can you send up a Chef's salad as soon as possible, please? I'm in a hurry.

Number 4

This is room 656. We'd like one ragôut and the cold roast beef, please.

Number 5

May we have one escalope, the 'Cordon Bleu', and a minute steak, please? It's room 100.

Number 6

Room 343 here. We'd like something to eat for the children please. The grilled sausages, for one, and a veal steak.

Number 7

A fried fish for my daughter, please, and minute steak for me. It's room 701.

Number 8

This is room 44. I'd like you to send up a tomato soup and a hamburger, please.

Key

1 b **2** c **3** a **4** c **5** a **6** c **7** b **8** c

9 MAKING SUGGESTIONS

You will now hear some guests. Choose the sentence in your book that answers the guest. Say the sentence onto the cassette. You will then hear the right answer. Here's the first guest.

GUEST: I'd like a main dish, but not a steak. What do you suggest?
YOU: Why don't you try the escalope 'Cordon Bleu', sir? It's excellent.

Number 2

GUEST: I'd like a salad, but I don't like beef.
YOU: Why don't you try the Chef's salad, sir? It's excellent.

Number 3

GUEST: I'd like a sweet after that. What have you got?
YOU: Why don't you try the ice cream, madam? It's on a fruit cocktail topped with whipped cream.

Number 4

GUEST: I'd like some soup, but not tomato or onion.
YOU: Why don't you try the consommé, madam? It's really very good.

Number 5

GUEST: Can you suggest something for my children? They're fussy eaters. I'm afraid they don't like fish and they won't eat anything like veal or escalope.

YOU: Why don't they try the sausages, madam? They're very good.

Number 6

GUEST: My children don't like meat. What do you suggest for them?

YOU: Why don't they try the fried fish, sir? It comes with French fries and a small mixed salad.

10 TAKE THE ORDER

Now listen to these guests. They are ordering meals. Look at the menu and write down the orders and the room numbers. Here's the first guest.

GUEST: Good evening. I'd like the tomato soup, followed by the ragôut of chicken, please. It's room 11.

Number 2

GUEST: Could you send up two consommés, one ragôut of chicken and a minute steak to room 44, please?

Number 3

GUEST: This is room 200. We'd like two cold roast beef salads, please, and one hamburger. And a bottle of red wine, your house wine, to go with it.

Number 4

GUEST: It's room 99. Something for my children, please. Two fried fish and a veal steak, and also three ice creams.

Number 5

GUEST: I'd like you to get me a 'Cordon Bleu' and a Chef's salad, please, and three veal steaks. We're in room 601.

Number 6

GUEST: A bottle of white wine, two Chef's salads, one grilled sausages and an ice cream, please. That's 205, the room number.

Key

For the key, look at the tapescript above.

Unit 4

1 WHAT DO YOU SAY?

1 c **2** f **3** b **4** d **5** a **6** e

2 SAYING WHAT YOU WILL DO

1 I'll get/ask/bring the wine waiter, madam.
2 I'll ask the chef about it, sir.
3 I'll get/bring you a clean one, sir.
4 I'll leave it in the cloakroom, sir.
5 I'll bring them to your table, sir.
6 I'll ask at reception for you, madam.
7 I'll get/bring the trolley, madam.
8 I'll get/bring another tablecloth, madam.

3 GIVING ADVICE

2 It's worth reserving a table, sir/madam. We get fairly full after 8 o'clock.
3 It's worth visiting our/the night club, sir/madam. There's a very good cabaret.
4 It's worth seeing the castle, sir/madam. There are some lovely views.
5 It's worth asking (at) reception, sir/madam. I'm sure they can help.
6 It's worth taking our/the courtesy bus, sir/madam. It runs every half hour.
7 It's worth trying the chef's speciality, sir/madam. It's really excellent.

4 ASKING WHAT THE GUEST PREFERS

1 Would you rather/prefer cognac or armagnac, sir?
2 Would you rather/prefer mixed vegetable or tomato, madam?
3 Would you rather/prefer red or white, madam?
4 Would you rather/prefer the entrecôte or the tournedos, madam?
5 Would you rather/prefer draught or bottled, sir?

5 OFFERING TO HELP

1 d 2 b 3 e 4 c 5 f 6 a

6 THE BREAKFAST MENU

Tapescript

Some guests are ordering breakfast. Listen to their orders. Then read the answers in your book. Listen to the order again and put a tick against the right order. Here's the first guest.

Good morning. I'll have the Continental breakfast, please.

Number 2
I'd like the American breakfast. Grapefruit juice, scrambled eggs with ham.

Number 3
The Healthy breakfast for me, please. With orange juice. Oh, and yoghurt, and tea.

Number 4
I'll take the orange juice, fresh that is, some coffee and a mushroom omelette, please.

Number 5
I'll have a hot chocolate, and poached eggs, please.

Number 6
The American breakfast for me. Tomato juice, and fried eggs with bacon.

Number 7
I'll have the Continental breakfast. Grapefruit juice, croissant and coffee, please.

Number 8
I'd like the Healthy breakfast. Let me see, yes, I'll have the tomato juice, oatmeal and caffeine free coffee. That'll do me nicely.

Key
1 b 2 a 3 c 4 a 5 c 6 c 7 c 8 c

8 WRONG ORDERS

You will now hear some guests. Choose the sentence that answers the guest. Say the sentence onto the cassette. You will then hear the right answer. Here's the first guest.

GUEST: I ordered orange juice, not tomato, you know.
YOU: I'll get you an orange juice immediately, sir.

Number 2
GUEST: I asked for yoghurt, not milk.
YOU: I'll fetch you a yoghurt straightaway, madam.

Number 3
GUEST: I wanted boiled eggs, not scrambled.
YOU: I'll get some boiled eggs immediately, sir.

Number 4
GUEST: I wanted a ham omelette, not a cheese one.
YOU: I'll ask chef for a ham omelette at once, madam.

Number 5
GUEST: What's this? I ordered coffee, not tea.
YOU: I'll get you some coffee straightaway, sir.

Number 6

GUEST: I think there's a mistake. Actually, I asked for fried eggs.

YOU: I'll fetch you some fried eggs at once, madam.

 ## 9 TAKE THE ORDER

Now listen to these guests. They are ordering meals. Look at the menu and write down the orders. Here's the first guest.

GUEST: I'll have the Healthy breakfast, please. Orange juice, oatmeal and tea.

Number 2

GUEST: I'd like the grapefruit juice, mushroom omelette. Oh, and coffee.

WAITER: With or without caffeine, sir?

GUEST: Without, thanks.

Number 3

GUEST: The Continental breakfast for me, please. Tomato juice, Danish pastry and tea.

Number 4

GUEST: My wife will have the American breakfast, please. Orange juice, poached eggs with sausage, toast and tea. And I'll have hot chocolate, scrambled eggs and, er, no, that's all, thank you.

Number 5

GUEST: Two American breakfasts, please, one with tomato juice, boiled eggs, toast and coffee. The other, grapefruit juice, poached eggs, a croissant and tea. OK?

Number 6

GUEST: We'll have two orange juices and a milk to drink, and, er, one fried eggs and bacon, one scrambled eggs and one ham omelette. And coffee for two, please.

Key

For the key, look at the tapescript above.

Unit 5

I HOW ARE THEY SERVED?

I d **2** f **3** b **4** e **5** a **6** c

2 HOW IS IT COOKED?

I No, sir/madam, they're boiled.
2 No, sir/madam, it's grilled.
3 No, sir/madam, they're poached.
4 No, sir/madam, it's baked.
5 No, sir/madam, it's whipped.

3 WHICH VEGETABLES?

I It's served with tomatoes, lettuce, cucumber, celery and beetroot, sir/madam.
2 They're served with onions, spinach and chips, sir/madam.
3 It's served with chips, broccoli and beans, sir/madam.
4 It's served with (roast) potatoes, carrots, peas and leeks, sir/madam.
5 It's served with (roast) potatoes, broccoli and peas, sir/madam.

4 WHERE WAS IT FOUND?

I Is this your purse, sir/madam? It was found on the table.
2 Are these your coats, sir/madam? They were left in the cloakroom.
3 Is this your wallet, sir? It was deposited at reception.
4 Is this your briefcase, sir/madam? It was discovered in the bar.
5 Is this your umbrella, sir/madam? It was handed in to the lost property office.
6 Is this your mackintosh, sir/madam? It was put over your chair.

5   A CHOICE OF VEGETABLES

Tapescript

Look at the list of vegetables in your book. Guests can choose which vegetables they want. Listen to the guests ordering their vegetables, and put a tick against the ones they want. Here's the first guest.

GUEST: And with the cold chicken, I'll have lettuce, tomatoes, runner beans and carrots, please.

Number 2

WAITRESS: And what would you like with the roast duck, madam?

GUEST: Let me see, er, roast potatoes, I think, spinach and brussels sprouts. Yes, that'll do fine, thank you.

Number 3

WAITER: What kind of salad would you like, sir?

GUEST: Celery, I love celery, and let's say beetroot, tomatoes and broad beans. That'll do me nicely.

Number 4

WAITRESS: And for vegetables, sir?

GUEST: Mushrooms, chips, peas and tomatoes, please.

Number 5

WAITER: Have you decided on your salad, madam?

GUEST: Yes. I'll take the lettuce, cucumber, beetroot and carrots, please.

Number 6

WAITRESS: What would you like as vegetables, madam?

GUEST: Let me see. Let's say leeks, boiled potatoes and some cauliflower.

Number 7

WAITER: And as a salad to go with that, madam?

GUEST: Something simple. Just tomatoes, broad beans and lettuce, please.

Number 8

WAITRESS: And what vegetables would you like with your roast lamb, sir?

GUEST: Cabbage, chips and, er, what about some broad beans. Oh, and some broccoli. I'm hungry this evening.

Key

For the key, look at the tapescript above.

7   MAKING SUGGESTIONS

These guests cannot decide what vegetables to have. Suggest what they should have, using the pictures in your book. First, listen to this example.

GUEST: What's good at the moment in the way of vegetables?

WAITER: I should have the broad beans and the spinach, sir. They're both in season at the moment.

Now you try that. Are you ready? Here's the first guest.

GUEST: What do you suggest at this time of year?

YOU: I should have the leeks and the brussels sprouts, madam. They're both in season at the moment.

Number 2

GUEST: What's your suggestion?

YOU: I should have the cauliflower and the peas, madam. They're both in season at the moment.

Number 3

GUEST: You choose what I should have.

YOU: I should have the runner beans and the cauliflower, sir. They're both in season at the moment.

Number 4

GUEST: What do you think I should have?

YOU: I should have the mushrooms and the spinach, madam. They're both in season at the moment.

Number 5

GUEST: Help me make up my mind, would you?

YOU: I should have the tomatoes and the runner beans, sir. They're both in season at the moment.

8 TAKE THE ORDER

Now listen to these guests. They are ordering vegetables. Write down the orders. Are you ready?

Number 1

GUEST: I'd like roast potatoes, peas and cabbage, please.

Number 2

GUEST: I'll have celery, tomatoes, lettuce and beetroot, please.

Number 3

GUEST: My husband will have chips, tomatoes and broad beans, and, er, let me see. Yes, I'll have boiled potatoes, cabbage and brussels sprouts.

Number 4

GUEST 1: I'll have the broccoli, with chips and peas. And my friends will have, er, what was it, George?

GUEST 2: Leeks and roast potatoes, if that's all right.

GUEST 1: Leeks and roast potatoes.

Number 5

GUEST: My son will have chips and tomatoes. I'll have broad beans and boiled potatoes. And my wife would like the cauliflower and roast potatoes. Thank you.

Number 6

GUEST: All three of us will have chips. And then it's one with peas and tomatoes, one with cauliflower and onions, and one with runner beans and brussels sprouts. Did you get that?

Key

For the key, look at the tapescript above.

Unit 6

1 GIVING MESSAGES

1 She says she's waiting in the bar.
2 He says he's expecting you in the lounge.
3 She says she's coming at 8 o'clock.
4 She says she's waiting on the verandah.
5 He says he's making a phone call.
6 She says she's arriving in half an hour.

2 MORE MESSAGES

2 Hello, Miss Pile. Mr Ogden says he'll be ten minutes late.
3 Hello, Mrs Renard. Mrs Singh says she'll wait in the lounge.
4 Hello, Mr Firth. Miss Andreotti says she'll be here in half an hour.
5 Hello, Mr Fouchet. Mr Short says he'll arrive at eight o'clock.
6 Hello, Miss Kleist. Mr Yamashta says he'll meet you in the foyer.

3 SAYING YOU'RE SORRY

1 I'm terribly sorry, Mr Robinson. Mrs Carmichael won't be able to have lunch with you today.
2 I'm terribly sorry, Mrs Chan. Miss Nilsson won't be able to have breakfast with you this morning.
3 I'm terribly sorry, Mr Jacques. Miss Henderson won't be able to meet you before lunch.

4 I'm terribly sorry, Mr Loewenthal. Mr Svensson won't be able to join you for dinner this evening.

5 I'm terribly sorry, Mr Schmidt. Mrs Li won't be able to meet you for drinks.

4   HOW DO YOU HELP THEM?

1 I'm very sorry, madam. I'll fetch a clean one immediately.

2 I'm very sorry, madam. I'll bring you some immediately.

3 I'm very sorry, madam. I'll tell the chef immediately.

4 I'm very sorry, madam. I'll get the wine waiter immediately.

5   THE LUNCH MENU

Tapescript

Some guests are ordering lunch. Listen to their orders. Then read the answers in your book. Listen to the order again and put a tick against the right answer. Here's the first guest.

I'd like the avocado vinaigrette to start with, please.

Number 2

And to follow that, I'll have the boeuf stroganoff.

Number 3

I just want a salad. The lobster mayonnaise, please.

Number 4

I'd like the gammon and apricot casserole, please.

Number 5

Some fish for me. The sole meunière, I think.

Number 6

Curry stuffed eggs to begin with.

Number 7

The veal escalope to follow.

Number 8

And I'll have the braised pork chops, thanks.

Key

1 b **2** c **3** a **4** a **5** b **6** a **7** b **8** c

7   TAKE THE ORDER

Now listen to these guests. They are ordering meals. Look at the menu and write down the orders. Here's the first guest.

I'd like the smoked salmon, please, followed by the goulash.

Number 2

I'll have the whitebait, and then the roast lamb. OK?

Number 3

It's one grapefruit, and one duck terrine and then a mixed vegetable salad, and the pork chops with orange.

Number 4

Two avocado vinaigrette, please, and one prawn cocktail. And after that, let's see, yes, it was two halibuts and a steak and mushroom pie.

Number 5

We'll have one duck terrine, one soup and whitebait. And to follow ... what was it? ... ah, yes, one salmon steak, one veal escalope, and a goulash.

Number 6

Just a Californian salad for my friend, but for me, I'll have the whitebait and then the trout with almonds, please.

Key

For the key, look at the tapescript above.

Unit 7

1 TELLING GUESTS WHAT TO DO

1 d **2** e **3** b **4** c **5** f **6** a

2 WHEN YOU CAN'T HELP

1 I'm sorry/afraid I can't help you, sir/madam. You'll have to wait until a table is free.
2 I'm sorry/afraid I can't help you, sir/madam. You'll have to deposit them at reception.
3 I'm sorry/afraid I can't help you, sir/madam. You'll have to ring his room.
4 I'm sorry/afraid I can't help you, sir/madam. You'll have to speak/go to the travel agent.
5 I'm sorry/afraid I can't help you, sir/madam. You'll have to go to the post office.
6 I'm sorry/afraid I can't help you, sir/madam. You'll have to speak to the manager.

3 HELPING THE GUEST

1 If you ask at reception, they'll be able to help you, sir.
2 If you like, I'll get the chef, sir.
3 If you're uncomfortable, I'll find you another table, sir.
4 If you take a seat, I'll bring your drinks to you, sir.
5 If you're ready, I'll take your order, sir.

4 PASSING MESSAGES

1 She said she would be in the bar, madam.
2 He said he would meet you at 8, madam.
3 He said he would wait in the foyer, sir.
4 She said she would arrive at 7.30, sir.
5 She said she would be in the lounge, sir.
6 He said he would come down immediately, madam.

5 THE DINNER MENU

Tapescript

Some guests are ordering dinner. Listen to their orders. Then read the answers in your book. Listen to the order again and put a tick against the right answer. Here's the first guest.

Now, to start with. I've had enough melon, and I had the sardines last night. So tonight I'll have the taramasalata.

Number 2
I fancy a little fish tonight. Not the mullet, it's too full of bones, and not halibut . . . er, I'll try the turbot.

Number 3
And my husband won't have any of those, but I know he'll like the kebabs.

Number 4
I love chicken. I'll have the coq au vin, please.

Number 5
I really would have liked a fillet steak, but I see it's not on the menu. So I'll try your beef with green peppers.

Number 6
Something light to follow, I think. Strudel's too heavy, and fruit salad I can't stand. The crême caramel.

Number 7
I'd like a German white wine. The Niersteiner, please.

Number 8
A bottle of the Chianti, please, and I hope it's a good one.

Key
1 a **2** b **3** c **4** b **5** c **6** a **7** c **8** b

7 TAKE THE ORDER

Now listen to these guests. They are ordering meals. Look at the menu and write down the orders. Here's the first order.

GUEST: My guest'll have the liver terrine, followed by the coq au vin, please. And I'll try the sardines and the sea bass.

Number 2

GUEST 1: It's one melon, one pâté and a consommé.

WAITER: Yes, sir.

GUEST 1: And to follow, roast turkey, a rump steak, medium rare, and yours was the veal casserole, wasn't it, Anne?

GUEST 2: No, not for me. I wanted the coq au vin.

GUEST 1: That's right. Sorry. Coq au vin, not veal casserole.

Number 3

GUEST: One melon, one taramasalata.

WAITRESS: Yes, madam.

GUEST: Then fish kebabs and chicken fricassée. And we'll have a bottle of Rosé d'Anjou to go with it.

WAITRESS: Certainly, madam.

Number 4

GUEST: Two vegetable soups and the sardines to start with.

WAITER: Yes, sir.

GUEST: And then one mullet, one spaghetti and a roast turkey after that.

WAITER: Thank you, sir.

GUEST: And I'd like to order the sweets now.

WAITER: If you like, sir, of course.

GUEST: Two rum gatêaux and a peach melba.

WAITER: Yes, sir.

Number 5

GUEST: I'd like the avocado, followed by the rump steak, please.

WAITRESS: Yes, madam.

GUEST: And my friend will have the liver terrine, then the beef with green peppers. And a bottle of Côtes du Rhône, please.

WAITRESS: Certainly, madam.

Number 6

GUEST: Two gin and tonics to start with, please. Aperitifs.

WAITER: Two gin and tonics, sir, yes.

GUEST: We'll start with two terrines.

WAITER: Yes, sir.

GUEST: The chicken fricassée, and veal casserole.

WAITER: Certainly, sir.

GUEST: With the appetizers, we'll have half a bottle of Entre-deux-Mers. And a bottle of Rioja with the main course.

WAITER: Thank you, sir. I'll get your aperitifs straightaway.

Key

For the key, look at the tapescript above.

Unit 8

I MAKING REQUESTS

1 f **2** e **3** b **4** c **5** a **6** d

2 WHEN DO YOU START?

2 We stop serving at 2 o'clock, sir/madam.

3 We start serving at 7 o'clock, sir/madam.

4 We stop serving at 10 o'clock, sir/madam.

5 We stop serving at 6 o'clock, sir/madam.

6 We start serving at 10 o'clock, sir/madam.

7 We start serving at 7 o'clock, sir/madam.

8 We stop serving at 10 o'clock, sir/madam.

3 WHAT DO YOU SAY?

1 I'll have/get it changed immediately, sir/madam.

2 I'll have/get it replaced immediately, sir/madam.

3 I'll have/get them moved immediately, sir.

4 I'll have/get them brought immediately, sir/madam.

5 I'll have/get it served immediately, sir/madam.

4 WHAT'S WRONG?

1 The tablecloth needs washing.

2 The tables need clearing.

3 The glass needs replacing.

4 The cutlery needs arranging.

5 The counter needs wiping.

6 The floor needs sweeping.

5 THE MENU

Tapescript

Some guests are ordering dinner. Listen to their orders. Then read the answers in your book. Listen to the order again and put a tick against the right answer. Here's the first guest.

I'll have a glass of white wine, please.

Number 2

A whisky on the rocks for me, please.

Number 3

I'll start with the oysters, please, and then the duck.

Number 4

The mushrooms, followed by the scallops for me.

Number 5

Soup and scampi, please.

Number 6

The tournedos, rare, please.

Number 7

I'll have the entrecôte, with peas, mushrooms and tomatoes.

Number 8

The herring salad and the venison will do me nicely, thank you.

Key

1 a **2** b **3** c **4** b **5** a **6** c **7** c **8** b

7 TAKE THE ORDER

Now listen to these guests. They are ordering meals. Look at the menu and write down the orders. Here's the first guest.

GUEST: I'd like a pastis first, please. Then I'll have the stuffed squid and then the escalope. With runner beans and chips.

Number 2

GUEST: Two Cinzanos to start with. Then one mussels and one herring salad. After that, one venison and rabbit. Both with peas, spinach and chips. Thank you.

Number 3

GUEST: One pâté and one antipasto. Then, what was it, ah yes, one Boeuf à la Bourguignonne with boiled potatoes and broccoli. And one scampi with chips.

Number 4

GUEST: A gin and tonic, and a whisky with water. Then I'll have the Salade Niçoise and my friend will have the soup. After that I'll have tournedos, with mushrooms, tomatoes and chips. And my friend will have lobster. By itself. Thank you.

Number 5

GUEST: Two Camparis, please. Then two oysters. After that I'll have scallops, no vegetables, and my friend will have the duck with roast potatoes and broad beans.

Number 6

GUEST: One sherry, one Dubonnet and a bourbon. Then one mushrooms in garlic butter, one squid and one herring salad. After that we'll have two entrecôtes, both with chips, tomatoes and peas. And one sole with cauliflower and boiled potatoes. Thank you.

Key

For the key, look at the tapescript above.

Unit 9

I   GIVING ADVICE

I d   **2** b   **3** c   **4** f   **5** a   **6** e

2   POLITE REQUESTS

I If you'd like to sit down, I'll bring your drinks to you.
2 If you'd like to give it to me, I'll take it to the cloakroom.
3 If you'd like to follow me, I'll show you to his table.
4 If you'd like to go up to the first floor, you'll find it on your left.
5 If you'd like to know the recipe, I'll ask the chef.
6 If you'd like to have some advice on wine, I'll send the wine waiter.
7 If you'd like to see the manager, I'll see if she's available.
8 If you'd like to wait a moment, I'll see if we have one free.

3   ANSWERING QUESTIONS

I It will/It'll be opening in ten minutes, madam.
2 It will/It'll be closing in an hour, madam.
3 It will/It'll be coming in a moment, madam.
4 They will/They'll be coming in two or three minutes, madam.
5 He will/He'll be arriving at 8 o'clock, madam.

4   ASKING QUESTIONS

I Certainly, sir. How many guests will you be bringing?
2 Certainly, sir. Where will you be waiting?
3 Certainly, sir. How will you be paying?
4 Certainly, sir. When will she be coming?
5 Certainly, sir. Where will you be sitting?

 ### 5   A MENU

Tapescript

Some guests are ordering lunch. Listen to their orders. Then read the answers in your book. Listen to the order again and put a tick against the right answer. Here's the first guest.

I don't really want any of these aperitifs here. What I'd really like is a nice, cool beer, on a hot day like this.

Number 2

A sherry for me, please. Dry.

Number 3

Prawns are one of my favourites. I'll have the king prawns.

Number 4

Now let's see. Something to start with. I'll try the pike mousse, as I haven't had that for years.

Number 5

Not moussaka today. I had that last night. I'll try the hare, I think.

Number 6

Chicken is what I'd like. I'll take the chicken chasseur.

Number 7

Spare ribs, please.

Number 8

Something filling, but not too filling. I'll have the goulash, thanks.

Key
1 b   2 a   3 c   4 a   5 c   6 a   7 a   8 a

 7   TAKE THE ORDER

Now listen to these guests. They are ordering meals. Look at the menu and write down the order. Here's the first guest.

I'd like a Campari first, please. Then I'll have melon, followed by the chicken chasseur.

Number 2

A pastis, please. Then I'll try the clams, followed by the Spanish pork, thanks.

Number 3

It's one whisky with water, no ice, and a vodka and orange. Then two mussels. No, sorry, one mussels and a pike mousse. After that we'll both have roast duck.

Number 4

A gin and tonic, an orange juice and a Cinzano, please. And for hors d'oeuvres it's one pâté and two shellfish cocktails. After that, an entrecôte, rare, one hare and one turbot with crab sauce, please.

Number 5

We'll both have a neat whisky, please. Neat, no water or ice. Then a consommé and the king prawns. After that I'll have the fillets of sole, and my friend will have the goulash. OK? Thanks.

Number 6

A rum, and a sweet sherry. After that we'll have the melon, followed by the mullet, and for me the clams and then the veal casserole. The children will both have melon, and then the chicken chasseur. Thank you.

Key

For the key, look at the tapescript above.

Unit 10

 I   THE BREAKFAST ORDER

Write down the guests' orders. Here's the first guest.

I'd like some scrambled eggs, some toast and coffee, please.

Number 2

I'll have a plain omelette, a grapefruit juice, a croissant and some tea, please.

Number 3

I'll take the vegetable salad, an orange juice and some coffee. Coffee without caffeine, that is.

Number 4

We'll have two poached eggs and a bacon omelette. Two yoghurts, coffee and toast for one, thanks.

Number 5

The children will both have oatmeal, a tomato omelette and chocolate. That's for the two of them. My wife will have boiled eggs and toast, and I'll have a ham omelette and a Danish pastry. My wife and I will have coffee.

Key

For the key, look at the tapescript above.

2 WHAT DO YOU SAY?

1 f 2 e 3 a 4 b 5 c 6 d

3 IN THE BAR

Some guests are ordering drinks. Write down the orders. Here's the first guest.

I'd like a malt whisky on the rocks, and a Bacardi and Coke, please.

Number 2

A regular vodka and orange, a malt whisky and a Campari, please.

Number 3

We'll have a Dubonnet, a glass of rosé wine and a gin and tonic, please.

Number 4

Two armagnacs, a Ricard and two Perrier waters. OK?

Number 5

An Irish whisky, a bourbon, a gin and tonic and a beer, please.

Number 6

We'll have two glasses of your champagne, a Cinzano with ice and lemon, a gin and water and a double malt whisky, please.

Key

For the key, look at the tapescript above.

4 THE MENU

Some guests are ordering meals. Write down the guests' orders. Here's the first guest.

I'll have the duck terrine to start with, please, and then the rump steak, medium rare, with French fries, mushrooms and peas.

Number 2

GUEST 1: We'll have the mussels and the pike mousse. And then, what was it for you, Anne? Ah, yes, the...

GUEST 2: Veal escalope.

GUEST 1: Ah, yes, the veal escalope.

GUEST 2: With runner beans and French fries.

GUEST 1: And for me, roast duck with roast potatoes, cauliflower, some brussels sprouts as well. Thank you.

Number 3

GUEST 1: The two children will have the melon and Parma ham to begin with, and I'll have the curried prawns. And what was it you wanted after that?

GUEST 2: The roast chicken.

GUEST 3: Me too.

GUEST 1: That's two roast chickens. They'll both have French fries and peas with it. And for me the goulash. With broccoli and boiled potatoes.

Number 4

GUEST: I'll have the soup of the day, the turkey salad and then a crème caramel. Thanks very much.

Number 5

GUEST 1: We'd like an aperitif to start with, please. A whisky on the rocks and a gin and tonic.

GUEST 2: The gin with ice and lemon, please.

GUEST 1: Then the consommé and the egg mayonnaise. Followed by the baked scallops, without any vegetables, and the hare. The hare with, let's see, leeks and broad beans.

Number 6

GUEST 1: We'll have an antipasto and three pâté maison. Then a mixed grill with tomatoes for me. And what was it for you?

GUEST 2: Spanish pork with French fries.

GUEST 3: Spare ribs. By themselves.

GUEST 4: Coq au vin, with French fries and runner beans for me. Thanks.

Key

For the key, look at the tapescript above.

GRAMMAR SUMMARY

Use this Grammar Summary to help you understand the exercises.

Unit 1

1 WHAT DO THEY DO?

The verb *to be*.
I am OR *I'm*; *you are* OR *you're*; *he/she/it is* OR *he's, she's, it's*; *we are* OR *we're*; *they are* OR *they're*.

The Present Simple
I work; *you work*; *he/she/it works*; *we work*; *they work*.
Remember to add *-s* or *-es* after he, she or it.
Use the Present Simple to talk about habits, for example,
I work in a hotel.
My friend goes to work by bus.

To ask a question, use *Do* (with I, you, we, they) or *Does* (with he, she, it) like this:
Do you speak English?
Does she work in the restaurant?

To make the negative, use *do not/don't* (with I, you, we, they) or *does not/doesn't* (with he, she, it), like this:
I do not/don't work in the bar.
She does not/doesn't speak English.

2 IN THE RESTAURANT

The verb *have got*.
I have got OR *I've got*; *you have got* OR *you've got*; *he, she, it has got* OR *he's, she's, it's got*; *we have got* OR *we've got*; *they have got* OR *they've got*.

3 WHAT DO YOU SAY?

You use *may* or *can* to ask the guest's permission for you to do something, like this:
Can (OR *May I*) *help you, sir?*

4 TELL THE GUEST THE WAY

Use a verb by itself when you are telling a guest what to do, like this:
Turn right, madam.
Ask at the front office, sir.

Unit 2

1 WHAT DO YOU SAY?

Use *Would you like to…?* when you want to invite the guest to do something, like this:
Would you like to sit down, madam?
Would you like to have a drink, sir?

2 ASKING QUESTIONS

These words help you ask questions: *when, where, what, how, who.*
Remember to use the question form after these words, like this:
I work in the bar.
*What time **do you begin** work?*

3 ANSWERING QUESTIONS

Look at Unit 1, Exercise 1: The Present Simple.

4 ANSWER THE GUESTS' QUESTIONS

The Past Simple
Use the Past Simple when you are talking about events that happened in the past.
To make the Past Simple, you usually add -d or -ed to the verb, like this:
I work (Present Simple)→*I work**ed*** (Past Simple).
Some verbs do not do this. They change, for example,
I go (Present Simple)→*I went* (Past Simple)

To ask a question about the past, use *Did*, like this:
Did you work last night?
Notice that when you use *Did* you do not add -d or -ed.
You do not use the past form of the verb.
Did you go to the cinema yesterday? (NOT Did you went…)

To make the negative, use *did not* or *didn't*, like this:
I did not/didn't work yesterday.
Again, do not use the past form of the verb.

6 SAYING *NO* POLITELY

Look at Exercise 4 above.

Unit 3

1 ASKING QUESTIONS

The Present Perfect
Use the Present Perfect when you are talking about events in the past which have a strong connection with the present.
I have lost my pen. (so now I can't write)
You also use the Present Perfect for events that started in the past but which are still continuing, like this:
I have worked in this hotel for five months. (and I am still working here)
To make the Present Perfect, use *have* or *has* and the participle. Most verbs have the same participle as their Past Simple, -d or -ed, for example,

PRESENT SIMPLE	PAST SIMPLE	PARTICIPLE	PRESENT PERFECT
I work	I worked	worked	I have worked He has worked

Some verbs change, like this:

PRESENT SIMPLE	PAST SIMPLE	PARTICIPLE	PRESENT PERFECT
I go	I went	gone	I have gone He has gone

To ask a question, change the order of *I have, The waiter has*, like this:
I have worked …
Have I worked …?
The waiter has worked …
Has the waiter worked …?

To make the negative, add *not*, like this:
I have not (or haven't) worked …
She has not (or hasn't) worked …

2 SOME MORE QUESTIONS

Look at Exercise 1 above.

3 WHAT'S THE BEST ANSWER?

Look at Exercise 1 above.

4 SOME SHORT ANSWERS

We usually answer questions using a short form. There are two ways to answer a question:
In a full sentence, like this:
Have you seen my briefcase?
Yes, I have seen your briefcase.
OR
No, I haven't seen your briefcase.
But we usually use a short answer, like this:
Have you seen my briefcase?
Yes, I have.
No, I haven't.
You usually repeat the verb the guest uses in his question, like this:
Can I see the manager?
Yes, you can.

5 HE MAY HAVE GONE TO RECEPTION

You use *may* and *could* to talk abut events that are possible, like this:
He may be in the bar. (It's possible he is in the bar, but I don't know.)
She could be in her room. (It's possible she is in her room, but I don't know.)
When you talk about a possible event in the past, you use *may/could*, then *have*, then the participle (*worked*, *gone* and so on), like this:
He may have left the hotel. (It's possible that he has left the hotel.)

6 TALKING TO GUESTS

You usually use words like this starting with *any-* and *no-* in negative sentences and in questions. You usually use words starting with *some-* in affirmative (yes) sentences.

Unit 4

1 WHAT DO YOU SAY?

You use *will* or *I'll* when you are promising to do something for a guest, like this:
I'll (OR I will) get the manager, madam.

2 SAYING WHAT YOU WILL DO

Look at Exercise 1 above.

3 GIVING ADVICE

You can use *worth* when you are giving a guest advice about what to do or see. Notice that after the word *worth* you must add *-ing* to the verb, like this:
It's worth visiting the old town.

4 ASKING WHAT THE GUEST PREFERS

You can use *prefer* or *rather* when you are giving the guest a choice.

5 OFFERING TO HELP

You can use *shall* when you are offering to help a guest.

Unit 5

I HOW ARE THEY SERVED?

The Present Simple Passive
You usually use the passive when what is done is more important than who does it, for example,
The chicken is fried.
Here what has happened to the dish is more important than who did it.
You make the Present Simple Passive by using *I am*, *You are*, *he/she/it is*, *We are*, *they are* and then the participle, like this:
It's grilled.
They're boiled.

2 HOW IS IT COOKED?

See Exercise I above.

3 WHICH VEGETABLES?

See Exercise I above.

4 WHERE WAS IT FOUND?

The Past Simple Passive
You make the Past Simple Passive by using *was/were* and the participle, like this:
The bill was paid by credit card.
They were found in the dining room.

Unit 6

I GIVING MESSAGES

When you give a message, you are often reporting what someone else has said. You can do this by using *he/she says …*

2 MORE MESSAGES

See Exercise I above.

3 SAYING YOU'RE SORRY

You use *will/won't be able to* as the future of *can*.
You can swim now. The pool is open.
You won't be able to swim tomorrow. The pool will be closed.

4 HOW DO YOU HELP THEM?

See Unit 4, Exercise I.

Unit 7

I TELLING GUESTS WHAT TO DO

You use *must* or *must not/mustn't* when you are giving a guest an order, like this:
You must leave at once, sir.

2 WHEN YOU CAN'T HELP

You use *will/'ll have to* when you are saying what the guest must do in the future. You can also use *must*, like this:
You must leave tomorrow, sir.
You'll have to leave tomorrow, madam.

3 HELPING THE GUEST

We call this Conditional 1. You can use Conditional 1 when you are offering to help a guest.
Notice that a Conditional 1 sentence has two parts. One starts with the word *if*.
You usually use the Present Simple in the *if*-part of the sentence, and *will*/*'ll* in the other part, like this:
*If you **like**, I **will**/**'ll** get the manager.*

4 PASSING MESSAGES

This is another way of reporting (Unit 6, Exercise 1).
Notice that when you use *he/she says* (in the Present Simple) you do not change the tense of the verb, like this:

GUEST: *Tell Mr Smith **I am** (Present Simple) in the bar.*

When you give the message, you say:

YOU: *Mr Smith says **he is** (Present Simple) in the bar.*

When you use *he/she said* (Past Simple) you must change the tense. There are rules for this.
will becomes *would*, like this:

GUEST: *Tell Mr Smith I'**ll** telephone him.*

When you give the message you say:

YOU: *Mr Smith said he **would** telephone you.*

Unit 8

1 MAKING REQUESTS

You can use *Would you mind...?* as a polite way of asking a guest to do something. Notice that after *Would you mind ...?* you must add *-ing* to the verb, like this:
Would you mind waiting a moment, madam?

2 WHEN DO YOU START?

After most English verbs you use *to*, for example,
*I want **to book** a table, please.*
After some English verbs you can use either *to* or you can add *-ing* to the verb, for example,
*We start **to serve** dinner at 8 o'clock.*
*We start **serving** dinner at 8 o'clock.*
After some verbs you must add *-ing*, for example,
*I enjoyed **staying** at your hotel.*
Verbs which must have *-ing* are:

> finish, prevent, risk, admit, delay, postpone, enjoy, forgive, pardon, excuse, suggest, keep (= continue), stop (= cease), understand, miss, involve, save.

There are others, but you will probably not need them.

3 WHAT DO YOU SAY?

You can use *will have* or *will get* and then the participle when you are promising to help a guest, but will not do it yourself, for example,
I'll get your room cleaned, madam. (Here, you won't clean the room yourself, but will make sure someone cleans it.)

4 WHAT'S WRONG?

Need is one of the verbs you can follow with *to* or you can add *-ing*. In Exercise 4 in Unit 8 add *-ing*.

Unit 9

I GIVING ADVICE

You can also use *If I were you* when you give a guest advice. Notice that in the second part of the sentence you use *would/'d* not *will* as in Conditional I, like this:
If I were you, I would/'d take a taxi, madam.

2 POLITE REQUESTS

This is a way to ask your guests questions politely. You use *If you'd like to . . . .* Notice that in the second part of your request you use *will*, like this:
If you'd like to tell me your name, I'll check your reservation.

3 ANSWERING QUESTIONS

This is the Future Continuous.
You use the Future Continuous for events that are about to happen in the near future, like this:
It'll be closing in five minutes, madam.
You make the Future Continuous with *will*, then *be* and then the verb with *-ing*.

4 ASKING QUESTIONS

You can also use the Future Continuous for future events that are planned, like this:
When will you be arriving, sir?
I'll be arriving at 8 o'clock.

Unit 10

There is no new Grammar in Unit 10.